POLITICS AND RELIGION CAN MIX!

POLITICS & RELIGION CAN MIX!

Claude A. Frazier

BROADMAN PRESS
Nashville, Tennessee

© Copyright 1974 • Broadman Press
All rights reserved
4289-19 (BRP)
4255-49 (Paperback)
ISBN: 0-8054-5549-3

Library of Congress Catalog Card Number: 74-79489
Dewey Decimal Classification: 261.7
Printed in the United States of America

To my uncle, Judge Alfred Frazier, who personifies the title of this book.

one of a family of seven children

sixty-two years a member of the South Knoxville Baptist Church

taught Sunday School classes several years

for several years, and is still, a member of the Board of Trustees of the church

graduated from the University of Tennessee, receiving the B.A. and LL.B. degrees (the latter was later conferred as Doctor of Jurisprudence)

was a judge of the Court of General Sessions in Knox County, Tennessee, for twenty-six years, having been elected four times to that office

married to Eula Jean, a daughter of the late Dr. A. E. Armstrong

Contents

Introduction

Spiritual guidelines are required by nations, families and individuals. Moral strength cannot be taken for granted.

Our nation, which includes each one of us, needs to turn to God and place its trust in him. "For thus saith the Lord God, the Holy One of Israel; 'In returning and rest you shall be saved; in quietness and in trust shall be your strength'" (Isa. 30:15, RSV).

I have heard many times over the past few months that government and religion can't mix. I believe religion and government can mix and *must mix* for our nation to survive.

I felt strongly that many of those who represent us in Washington and in state houses are men of deep religious faith and would be willing to give a personal testimony of their faith. When I wrote them requesting they do this, I was not disappointed. These leaders are not ashamed to confess their faith before men. We should be proud to have persons as our leaders. I feel more secure to have them guide our nation. (The testimonies of these leaders appear as they have given them with only slight editorial changes.)

Our nation was founded upon Christian principles. The Mayflower Compact in 1620, the Declaration of Independence of 1776, and the Consitution of 1789 give recognition to God. The Declaration and the Constitution were proclaimed in Independence Hall in Philadelphia. Here also hangs the Liberty Bell. Around its crown are the words from the twenty-fifth chapter of Leviticus, "Proclaim Liberty Throughout All the Land Unto All the Inhabitants Thereof."

Our country was established and has been sustained by men of faith. A clergyman was a signer of the Declaration of Independence. The patriotic hymn "My Country 'Tis of Thee" was written by a clergyman. Another clergyman authored the Pledge of Allegiance to the Flag.

"In God We Trust" is our motto. But do we have trust in him? Do we not place more confidence in the dollar on which the motto is engraved? God alone is worthy of our trust.

Man's deep need is to place his trust in God. There is no adequate foundation for a life or country apart from unwavering faith in God. Trust in God is a personal need. Our country is made up of individuals—you and me. Each of us needs to turn to God and surrender to his will.

It is the moral fiber of any nation found rooted in its individual citizens which determines the heights to which any nation can aspire. It has been said that men without principles are dangerous, but principles without men are useless.

True, we love our country. But have we expressed it by our actions? This is *our* country. This is *our* own native land.

Let us be jealous of its honor, rejoice in its strength and its path into the future. The future is in the hands of God.

History is a forward-looking process. A Christian's view of history is optimistic. History is going somewhere according to the purpose of God.

Let us truly be a nation *under God!*

I want to express my appreciation to Miss Kathy Stirewalt, my secretary, whose effort, patience, and endurance helped bring this book to its final stage. I would also like to thank each contributor for their cooperation and assistance with this book.

CLAUDE FRAZIER, M.D.

Asheville, North Carolina

Foreword

At this time in our history many people are asking the question whether anybody in politics can be trusted. Indeed, the pollsters have concluded that the American voters have a very low view of their elected officials. And what is true in the nation's Capitol is true in the state capitols as well.

Dr. Claude Frazier has edited a collection of statements by a variety of government officials from many political walks of life. His purpose is to show that one can be truly religious and still be engaged in politics. In years gone by no one would have disputed this notion, for many fine Christian people devoted their lives to service in the political life of our nation. Increasingly, however, America has been moving in the direction of secularism and even many people who have had the benefit of a religious environment and heritage have not themselves had any dynamic religious experience. But this does not mean there are no real Christians in government. Indeed, the situation is probably better than most people suppose.

In Washington, the International Christian Leadership, founded by Abraham Vereide, has hosted the presidential prayer breakfasts and has worked indefatigably among the members of the House and the Senate, through prayer meetings, Bible study groups, and personal witnessing. There are many prayer and Bible study groups that meet regularly for the thousands of government employees in the Washington area. There is a prayer meeting that convenes in the White House itself and attracts born-again Christians concerned for the nation. Ministers of the gospel, like Richard Halverson of the Fourth Presbyterian Church of Bethesda, Maryland, have a significant witness and impact in the nation's capital.

Chaplain of the Senate, Dr. Edward L. R. Elson, was long-time minister of the National Presbyterian Church. Senator John Stennis, who was shot by a robber and barely escaped with his life, is a member of that great congregation now led by Louis Evans, Jr. There are committed Christians in politics who are members of this and other churches in the Washington area.

Dr. Frazier has gathered statements from a number of men and women in political life who have shared their religious convictions. They will be of interest to Americans everywhere. These statements vary widely and make clear the disparate theology of the authors. There are some statements with which I would be in general agreement; there are others that differ widely from what I myself believe. But what is important is that they do tell us what the religious convictions of some of our leaders are, whether they represent our convictions or not.

It would be foolish as well as sub-Christian for followers of Jesus Christ to eschew politics because of its current unpopularity. We need more Christian politicians than ever before. We need Christians with the highest ethical standards who will bring new life to our system. We need people who will not hesitate to vote their convictions, who will not commit unlawful acts, and whose lives will be characterized by an unimpeachable integrity.

There can be no doubt that it is possible for men and women to mix politics and religion. But this can be done only when their politics are informed by their Christian convictions. In other words, the political life must be built on a Christian foundation that puts biblical principles before expediency and makes decisions consonant with Christian ethical precepts. This has been accomplished in American life in days gone by, it is being done by some outstanding Christians now, and it can be done again in the days ahead by Christians who are willing to pay whatever price is demanded and whose commitment remains unsullied.

HAROLD LINDSELL
Editor-Publisher, *Christianity Today*

A Word from Senator Hugh Scott of Pennsylvania

Our affirmation as "one nation, under God" recognizes no state religion, but emphasizes our dependence upon our faith in a Supreme Being. Without such faith our legislative efforts would lack compassionate recognition of the worth of the human being created in God's image.

While the religion of each legislator is private to himself, the force of religious principles transforms legislative concerns from what would otherwise be sere and barren service to actions in which the recognition of divine precepts is implicit.

Governor Reubin Askew of Florida

Aside from my personal and family life and my involvement in our local congregation, I like to think that my Christian commitment has been expressed in professional public service.

It is my conviction that our lives should not be carefully compartmentalized, but rather that our trust in and loyalty to God should be the integrating factor in our day-to-day living—family, education, and career, politics included. I have often stated that, while I believe in the separation of church and state, I do not believe in the separation of church and statesman. Neither do I see a sharp distinction between religious commitment and matters of citizenship.

In the wake of recent events in Washington and in a time in which many of the problems which beset us seem so overwhelming, I am concerned with what seems to be a failure of civic nerve—a crisis of the spirit in our land. There seems to be a tendency toward disillusionment and even despair on the part of many Americans. Too many good and decent citizens seem to wonder if activity in the public arena is really worth the effort.

Recent polls indicate that the people's faith in their government has declined sharply. Many citizens feel discouraged about their ability to have any effect on the shaping of public policy.

Such a sense of discouragement and the cynicism it often generates constitute the greatest single threat to our democratic process. For without faith in self-government and active participation in the political process our system simply cannot work.

In the first century, Paul advised Christians in Rome to have a positive attitude toward government and encouraged obedience to those in authority. In our Republic today obedience is still important, but now it is given because our system is based upon the consent of the governed. That consent, however, cannot be really meaningful and effective without an informed and involved citizenry.

The wisdom of the democratic way of government is deeply rooted in our Judeo-Christian tradition. The founding fathers of our Republic were committed to the proposition that no person or small group of leaders is either wise or good enough to control others, except as they are specifically delegated to do so by the people.

In our time the great American theologian Reinhold Niebuhr expressed Christian insight, tempered by realism, when he said: "Man's capacity for justice makes democracy possible; but his inclination to injustice makes democracy necessary."

The United States Constitution reflects biblical realism in its recognition of human nobility as well as human weakness.

The founding fathers rejected the proposition of the divine right of human rulers and assumed that ultimate power is God's alone and therefore governmental power should be carefully limited and balanced. All political power was to be accountable to the people.

The idea of accountability to God and the people is at least as old as the prophetic tradition in Israel in which Nathan, the Lord's prophet, dared to say to King David that there are acts that even a monarch cannot do without incurring judgment.

Perhaps the most important way in which government can become more responsive and accountable to the people it serves is through vigorous activity on the part of interested citizens who together represent the common interest and the common good. I believe we need a revival of civic courage. Much of our difficulty today is the result of our too timid faith in democracy. Our problems are not insoluble so long as we do not experience a failure of nerve.

The God in whom we place our faith grants us courage in the struggle for justice and human fulfillment and sustains us in periods when much is demanded from us. Our part is to believe that we can find answers in time of adversity and that our involvement is worth the effort.

To claim to be a Christian or Jew who loves God and neighbor and not to take an active part in the formation of just social policies affecting those neighbors would seem to deny complete fulfillment of one's faith. Just as you cannot or should not separate religious commitment from citizenship, I do not believe in separating religious conscience from those who might make public policy.

I think it's the duty of every believer who holds public office to try to be true to that conscience. It is a conscience that seeks peace in the land and in the world. It is a conscience that shows compassion for the needy and the under-represented. It is a conscience that deals honestly and responsively with the people who more than ever want and deserve political leadership they can trust.

Our religious communities also have a responsibility to participate in the revitalization of American life. Their basic and primary function, however, must always be the fostering of great individual faith and personal salvation.

It has been argued that the most significant ethical issue of our time is that of our ultimate loyalties. And the essence of morality, personal integrity and, indeed, salvation is loyalty to the worthiest of causes.

It is here that our religious communities play their most crucial role. As important as our loyalties to self, to family, to profession and country are, our overriding loyalty must be to God and his cause. Our biblical tradition identifies that cause as "the Kingdom of God."

I believe that it is our churches and synagogues which must constantly call us to courageous and constant loyalty to God and his cause. This is their fundamental ministry and the purpose for their existence.

Without such a focus, we will flounder as a people—"Where there is no vision, the people perish."

Yet this loyalty, and this vision, must manifest itself in helping God's people. For the ultimate test of our faith is in the living of it.

Reubin O'Donovan Askew was elected Governor of Florida in 1970 as essentially a tax reform candidate.

He has received honorary degrees from the University of Notre Dame, Stetson University, Rollins College, and Florida Southern College. Among Askew's earlier honors was his selection by the State Jaycees in 1960 as "One of Florida's Five Outstanding Young Men." He now serves as Chairman of the Education Commission of the States and Vice-Chairman of the Southern Governor's Conference.

His many community services include being a past president of the Western Division of Children's Home Society of Florida, past member of the Board of Directors of the Florida Association for Retarded Children, the Farm Bureau, Escambia County Tuberculosis and Health Association, YMCA, American Legion, Heart Association, and United Fund.

Born in Muskogee, Oklahoma, on September 11, 1928, Governor Askew was one of six children.

He is married to the former Donna Lou Harper of Stanford, Florida, and the couple has two children, Angela Adair and Kevin O'Donovan. Governor Askew is an elder in the First Presbyterian Church of Pensacola.

Governor Dale Bumpers of Arkansas

It is faith that has sustained and kept the universe alive. Ever since the beginning of the human species, man has made his slow progress through faith in himself and in what he could accomplish for the good of his fellowman.

It was faith on the part of a Burbank that could take the wild dog rose and convert it into an American Beauty which ravishes the eye. It was faith that converted howling wildernesses into teeming, thriving, growing cities. It was faith that man could discover natural law and through its operation enable him to stand on the moon. It is faith in myself and what I can accomplish that has sustained me through the years. What is there in this simple trust in myself, in this confidence I have in a person or a thing that gives meaning, power, and significance to my life and which brings me increasing security, stability, and poise?

First, I have a great trust in the over-arching guidance of a Higher Power than myself. Theologians have called it God. Scientists have named it the First Cause; metaphysicians, Supreme Intelligence. No matter how one denominates it, as long as there is a power greater than myself that gives meaning, purpose, significance to myself, I can keep going.

Trained as I have been in the schools of organized religion, I believe firmly in God and to him I daily turn for renewed strength and sustenance to allow me to go through each day's routine knowing that a just and loving God is watching over me. And when each day is over and I have wangled over social, economic, and political issues and have brushed shoulders with legislators, businessmen, professional persons, the poor and the needy, I can close my eyes and with the poet exclaim:

> My spirit I commit to Him
> My body too, and all I prize.
> Both when I sleep and when
>   I wake.
> He is with me, I shall not
>   fear.

Secondly, I have great faith in the ideals I cherish. I have always been a great admirer of Plato, the Greek thinker whose philosophy has been patterned after the ideal republic—a republic in which love and justice, harmony and peace would rule the hearts of one's fellowmen. Therefore, I have always strived to let these virtues govern my everyday activities. No one ever completely realizes his dreams, his visions, his hopes, for they out-distance him. Nonetheless, one must strive to translate his aspirations into concrete daily living.

No one is asked to complete the ideals he cherishes in his lifetime, but he is not free to desist from pursuing them. Therefore, happy is the man who knows that his dreams out-distance the reality of his being, but who nonetheless pursues them. Supreme among the ideals I have always charished is the perfectability of man, that he is able to build a nobler, a grander and a statelier universe than the one bequeathed to him by his ancestors.

Consequently, I have always held that my neighbor possesses the same dignity of personality that I do. And since we are all children of the same God, I owe my neighbor in whom I have great faith, all the nobility of mind and character I possess. Wherever I go, whatever I do, I believe in the dignity of the individual. This is the highest ideal I can cherish, and to it I must dedicate the years of my life—to accord my fellow-comrade on life's highway the dignity of personality to which I pray he may ever reciprocate in his relations with me.

Thirdly, and lastly, I have an abiding faith in the efficacy of the moral law—those moral imperatives by which all men must live and conduct their lives. Those moral imperatives are embodied in the Ten Commandements, in the nine beatitudes, in the Golden Rule, and for the state to survive and grow, it must be built upon these moral imperatives.

I should conduct the affairs of the state so that I should not lie, nor steal, nor bear false witness, but love my neighbor as I do myself. These moral truths are part and parcel of my very being, and because I have faith in the efficacy of these moral mandates, I have always strived to live my life and conduct the affairs of the state so as to confer nobility and honor upon the office to which I have been elected. Noblesse oblige—nobility obligates me to excellence in office, in personal affairs, and in matters of statecraft. In this philosophy of living, I fervently believe and dedicate the years of my life. God grant me the strength to live by this faith so that when I shall have been gathered unto my Father, the generation of which I have been part and parcel and in which I have given the dedication of my years may say of me: "Well done, thou good and faithful servant."

Dale Bumpers was born August 12, 1925, in Charleston, Arkansas. He is married to Betty Flanagan Bumpers. They have two sons: Brent, age 20, and Bill, age 17; one daughter, Brooke, age 11.

He graduated from the University of Arkansas and the Northwestern Law School with an L.L.B. in 1951.

Governor Bumpers is a member and lay teacher of Charleston United Methodist Church, and a member, Council of Ministeries. He is lay leader for the Fort Smith, Arkansas, District of the United Methodist Church. He served in the United States Marine Corps, Pacific Theatre during World War II and received an honorable discharge in 1946.

Dale Bumpers was owner of Charleston Hardware and Furniture Company from 1951 to 1966; owner of Angus Breeding Farm from 1966-1970; city attorney for Charleston, Arkansas, and in private law practice from 1951 to 1970. He has served as president of Charleston Chamber of Commerce; past chairman, United Fund, Boy Scout Fund, Cancer Fund; past president of Charleston School Board. He received the Chamber of Commerce Citizens' Award. He also served as Special Justice on Arkansas Supreme Court.

Governor Jimmy Carter of Georgia

I am a farmer by profession. I am a nuclear physicist by education. And I am a governor temporarily.

I have no particular qualifications to be a preacher nor to judge others. But I do have a strong inclination and feeling of responsibility as a layman and as a recipient of the Lord's grace to witness my faith in God to my fellowman.

The most important thing in my life is Jesus Christ. I turn to him in prayer daily and before every decision I have to make which affects the lives of others. And as in every other person's life, I am constantly faced with decisions in all areas of my life which will have an impact on the lives of others.

I am a father and love my children . . . and I am a Christian.

I am a businessman . . . and I am a Christian.

I am a politician . . . and I am a Christian.

I don't believe there is any inherent conflict between these roles. There is no wedge that need separate a man from his commitment to his family, his neighbors, his customers, his clients, and his fellowmen and his commitment to Christ.

The only potential conflict we all face is one that we create ourselves—one caused when we are not willing to

relinquish worldly prestige, possessions, and social prominence in order to grasp without reticence the hand of God.

I remember a minor episode that occurred during my childhood as a farmboy. We lived across the road from the Seaboard railroad track and had no electricity or running water. Like all other boys, I always carried around a slingshot. The little round, white stones on the roadbed of the railroad track gave me a ready supply of ammunition.

I remember very well—one day I was out on the railroad track, and I had filled my pockets, as well as my hands, with rocks and headed back toward the house when my mother called me from the front porch. As I walked up to her, she offered me some cookies from the plateful she had just baked. I stood there twenty, maybe thirty, seconds, not knowing how to take the cookies with my hands full of rocks. And it took quite a while before I decided to drop those worthless rocks and to take the cookies that my mother had baked for me with heart full of love!

This simple conflict is a good example of those that we as businessmen or farmers or nuclear physicists or politicians are faced with daily: Do we cling to the rocks without properly assessing the relative value of what is offered to us?

We, as Americans, in this tough, competitive world, have learned to be aggressive, manly, and unafraid. Because of this, we have developed a pride in our own toughness and thus our priorities have sometimes become distorted.

I learned the danger of such a false pride several years ago through an experience in Springfield, Massachusetts, with a Cuban minister named Eloy Cruz.

We had both been asked to go to Springfield to witness to a community of Spanish-speaking people. Although I had learned to speak Spanish in the Navy, I felt unprepared to give my life totally to God for a full week, with no strings attached, because I had never before done that.

In Springfield we visited in home after home and talked to people who were bereft of friendship, who could not speak the language, who gathered in groups to watch the television and turned off the sound because they couldn't understand what was being said. They lived in the most poverty-stricken ghetto area of Springfield. As we visited, I watched my friend, Eloy Cruz, a broad-shouldered, swarthy man who was the epitome of masculine strength but who could convince the people that he was equally sinful as they and that God loved them as much as he loved us.

The last day, we had an unusually moving experience with a young man whose eighteen-year-old wife had died in the dentist's chair because of unaccountable and uncontrollable bleeding. This young man, who was fairly well educated, had tried to commit suicide and kill his little baby.

Although he was at first hesitant to let us into his home, he finally agreed to talk to us. And after a long discussion, Bible reading in Spanish, and prayer, he ultimately accepted Christ.

As I came down the stairs of that tenement house with tears running down my cheeks, I turned to Eloy Cruz to tell him good-bye, for he was returning to Brooklyn to his church, and I was returning to Georgia. And with a great outpouring of admiration, I asked him, "Senor Cruz, how is it that you, a tough, strong, forceful man, are so able to touch those people's hearts with such compassion, love, and understanding?"

He answered me, "Senor Jimmy, you have to remember this. Our Savior has hands that are very tender, and he can't do much with a man who is hard."

In our tough, manly, powerful, and proud ways, we sometimes have difficulty hearing Christ knocking on the door of our hearts, asking to come in and permeate our lives with his presence. We tend to think that because we attend church, help our neighbors, and contribute to charity that we will be saved by God for our good works.

How far this is from the truth.

We are saved by his grace.

I pray that I will be ever mindful of this, that remembering my own inadequacies, I will constantly be open to the presence of the Holy Spirit. I pray too that all those who have been entrusted by their fellowman to positions of leadership will be guided and blessed by the Lord to set examples of honesty, integrity, compassion, understanding, truthfulness, and love.

Jimmy Carter became Georgia's seventy-sixth governor on January 12, 1971. He was born and grew up in the small farming town of Plains in the southwest corner of Georgia.

In 1966 he ran for governor of Georgia and was narrowly defeated. In 1970 he ran again and was elected by a margin of more than two to one. He graduated from the United States Naval Academy, and while he did his service in the Navy was stationed all over the world.

In his inaugural address Governor Carter promised that

no Georgian would ever again be deprived of a job, an education, or simple justice because he was poor, rural, black, or not influential.

He has been elected by fellow governors to serve as chairman of the Southern Regional Education Board comprising fourteen states, the Appalachian Regional Commission comprising thirteen states, and the Coastal Plains Regional Commission comprising three states.

Carter was recently appointed to chair the Campaign '74 Committee for the National Democratic Party by Chairman Robert Strauss.

Senator Carl T. Curtis of Nebraska

Faith is a growing thing. It is not static.

It is difficult to put down in a concise statement the reasons for one's faith, because tomorrow and next year there will be additional reasons why I believe.

The eternal truths of Christianity are supported by everything that happens.

In the first place, I believe that there has to be a Creator. Just as there can't be a garden without a gardener. This marvelous universe in which we live had to be created.

Man was created. This earth of ours is a beautiful, productive place for birds and animals and man to enjoy. So far as we know, no other planet has air to breathe, or water, or life.

Man was created. Our Declaration of Independence begins with the words, "We hold these truths to be self-evident, that all men were created." All creation is great beyond our ability to describe. The human body is the most marvelous functioning machine that anyone could imagine. The laws of the universe are fixed and dependable. Our astronauts and everybody else can count on them.

For someone to contend that all this wonderful creation just happened to evolve would be ridiculous. Such a person would have to believe in fantastic miracles far beyond anything recorded in sacred Scripture. The fact that growth

and change take place does not explain away the necessity that there had to be a Supreme Mind, a Designer, a Creator.

It is perfectly logical for man to ask: "If God exists, why does he keep man guessing as to his existence? Why doesn't he show himself?" The answer to that question leads me to my second reason as to why I believe.

God has just done that very thing. He has revealed himself to man. The Christian religion is not man-made. It is not the result of man's noblest thoughts and his grasping for the infinite. *God has revealed himself to man.* The Scriptures are replete with such revelation. The Old Testament is a continuous story not of man reaching for God, but God revealing himself to man.

The Bible stands as a true revelation of God to man. I am not unaware that the critics and scholars raise questions about the accurate scientific background of certain accounts that appear in the Bible. But I am not the least impressed or disturbed by them. I will tell you why.

Last night, as I got the news on television, the weather forecaster told me what time the sun would rise and what time it would set. This morning when I picked up my newspaper, I read that the sun would set at such and such a time and rise at such and such a time. Now that was not true at all. Everybody knows that the sun does not rise and set at all. Yet the conveyance of information about daylight and darkness to me in language I could understand does not mean that news report that I heard over the television or the news which I read in my paper were not accurate accounts of what happened in the world yesterday.

The revelations appearing in the Old Testament are but

half the story. Christ came to the earth to reveal God, to show man just what God was like, and what he had in mind for man. It is not at all hard for me to accept the belief that Christ is divine, that *Christ is God.*

His earthly life was flawless. His teachings are flawless. Whenever his teachings are followed, everything goes all right. When his teachings are ignored, things go wrong. That proves that his teachings are eternal. Daniel Webster declared that the Sermon on the Mount could not be a mere human production.

The image of God that Christ brought to earth—which shows the Father as a Father concerned about every human being—is a flawless image. That image could only fit an omnipotent, all-wise, all-powerful Creator.

There are those who have an intellectual struggle in an effort to believe that Christ had to die for the salvation of men. They would picture Christ's death as an appeasement to a revengeful God who had to kill somebody because of man's sins.

I do not believe that Christ died because God had to take his revenge out on somebody. I would point out to those who are troubled about the crucifixion of Christ being a part of God's plan that Christ's saving mission was two-fold: (1) to show man what God was like; and (2) to show man what God's plans for the human race were.

If Christ was to teach man how to live, the most effective way was to come to earth and live like man. This was done. He was born, he grew up. He lived on earth and he taught. A very important part of his teaching was that life was eternal, that there was a life beyond the grave. Is there a better way to teach that than by example?

There had to be a resurrection in order to teach the principle of eternal life. And there can be no one resurrected from the dead unless the person is dead. Therefore, Christ died for men so that he might be resurrected and thus reveal to man the infinite plan and purpose of God.

The third reason why I believe in God and in Jesus Christ is that all history proves God's existence. He is the God of history. As I read the history of nations and of men, I see his plan at work. We know that Christianity is true *because it works.* If it were false or if it were based upon false claims, it would not work. It does work.

An account is related concerning a civilization that once possessed a formula for concrete. The formula was lost for several generations. It was finally rediscovered. How did they know that they had discovered the original and true formula? They knew because it worked. It cemented things together and held firm. We know that Christianity is true because it works.

When Christ said, "I am the Way," it might be asked "The way to do what?" The answer is, "The way to do anything."

What is the best way for people to get along with one another? What is the best way for parents to treat children and children to treat parents? What is the best way to run a political campaign or a business? What is the best way to treat the unfortunate, the lonely, the sorrowing, and the destitute?

The answer is—the Christian way—that is the way to do anything. It is the right way because it works.

It might well be contended that all the foregoing reasons that I have given as to why I believe are intellectual reasons based upon the experience of others. Therefore, I want to go a step farther. I believe in God and in Jesus Christ as God because I have that feeling within.

I have experienced him. He has guided me and helped me beyond my expectations and far beyond that which I deserve. He has consoled me and strengthened me. In time of trial, he has saved me from trouble. He has answered my prayers even though I do not understand why sometimes he has answered with a no. I believe, however, that he knows best.

I do not make these claims because of any miraculous happening in my life. There has been no burning bush, no quaking of the earth. I have come to believe in Christ and accept him in response to all the instruction that I have received since my childhood. And my faith, based upon the witness within me, grows greater every day.

Although I haven't one iota of musical ability myself, I know of no one who loves great hymns more than I do. One of my favorites is "How Great Thou Art." It was first written by Reverend Carl Boberg—in Sweden about 1885—who, although he was a great preacher and religious editor, served for fifteen years as a Senator in the Swedish Parliament. Here is how it goes:

> O Lord my God, when I in awesome wonder
>   Consider all the worlds Thy hands have made,
> I see the stars, I hear the rolling thunder,
>   Thy pow'r thro'out the universe displayed.
>
> When through the woods and forest glades I wander
>   And hear the birds sing sweetly in the trees,
> When I look down from lofty mountain grandeur,
>   And hear the brook and feel the gentle breeze.

And when I think that God, His Son not sparing,
    sent Him to die, I scarce can take it in,
That on the cross, my burden gladly bearing,
    He bled and died to take away my sin.

When Christ shall come with shout of acclamation
    and take me home, what joy shall fill my heart!
Then I shall bow in humble adoration,
    And there proclaim, my, God, how great Thou art.

REFRAIN:
    Then sings my soul, my Saviour God, to Thee;
        how great Thou art, how great Thou art!
    Then sings my soul, my Saviour God, to Thee,
        How great Thou art, How great Thou art!

Senator Curtis has been a Member of Congress continuously since January 3, 1939. He entered the Senate on January 1, 1955. His present term will expire January 3, 1979. He was elected to the United States House of Representatives for eight consecutive terms. He is the dean of the Nebraska Delegation in Congress.

The Senator was born near Minden, Nebraska, on March 15, 1905. He attended Nebraska Wesleyan University. He holds honorary L.L.D. degrees. He practiced law in Minden and was prosecuting attorney for Kearney County.

Carl Curtis was married on December 1, 1972, to Mrs. Mildred Baker of Palo Alto, California.

He is a member of Masonic bodies, the Shrine, the Nebraska Bar Association, Rotary, Elks, Odd Fellows, and Theta Chi Fraternity and an honorary member of Phi Delta Phi Legal Fraternity and Pi Kappa Delta Forensic Fraternity. He is a member of the Presbyterian Church of the U.S.A.

Senator Sam J. Ervin, Jr., of North Carolina

As a member of the Senate group, I am deeply grateful to International Christian Leadership for the privilege it affords me each week to lay aside for a time, the burdens of office and join colleagues in meditation upon the everlasting things.

I wish to speak of two of the everlasting things—faith and courage. The Bible defines faith "as the substance of things hoped for, the evidence of things not seen." It entreats us to "be of good courage,"

The canny Scotchman, Thomas Carlyle, made a profound observation when he said: "A man lives by believing something; not by debating and arguing many things." As the evidence of things not seen, faith proves to men and women the reality of the positive beliefs by which they live and for which they are willing to die.

Faith is not a storm cellar to which men and women can flee for refuge from the storms of life. It is, instead, an inner force which gives them the strength to face those storms and their consequences with serenity of spirit. In times of greatest stress, faith has the miraculous power to lift ordinary men and women to greatness.

Faith is exhibited at its best in the lives of those men and women who trust the promises of God. At a time when her physical eyes were failing, Annie Johnson Flint saw these promises with the eyes of faith, and described them for us in her inspiring little poem entitled, "What God Hath Promised."

God hath not promised	But God hath promised
Skies always blue,	Strength for the day,
Flower-strewn pathways	Rest for the labor,
All our lives through	Light for the way,
God hath not promised	Grace for the trials
Sun without rain,	Help from above,
Joy without sorrow,	Unfailing sympathy,
Peace without pain.	Undying love.

Fear has been the devastating enemy of mankind in all generations.

In considering this subject, we must be careful to distinguish between fear, which is foolish, and a somewhat related emotion, anxiety, which is wise. Anxiety causes one concern about future events likely to occur and induces him to take provident steps to prepare for them. Fear fills one with dread of dangers which are imaginary or dangers which cannot be avoided.

People are probably more fearful today than they were at any time in the past. They are assailed on all sides by the old fears, such as fear of economic insecurity, fear of loss of status, fear of sickness, and fear of death, Moreover, they are haunted by a new terror, the fear of annihilation in a war fought with atomic or hydrogen weapons. As a consequence, the state of many people is similar to that of the singing stevedore in Oscar Hammerstein's lyric "Ol' Man River."

> I gits weary and sick of tryin'
> I'm tired of livin' an' feard of dyin'.

If we are to overcome the fears which beset us, we must have courage.

Joanna Baillie described courage aright in this verse:

> The brave man is not he who feels no fear,
> For that were stupid and irrational;
> But he, whose noble soul its fear subdues,
> And bravely dares the danger nature shrinks from.

Courage falls into two categories. These are physical courage, which enables one to brave physical dangers, and moral courage, which empowers one to carry the burdens and take the heavy blows of life without losing heart.

Let us consider briefly how we can develop courageous personalities that will enable us to scorn dangers which are imaginary and defy dangers which cannot be avoided.

One way is to live a day at a time. As Robert Louis Stevenson said: "Anyone can carry his burden, however hard, until nightfall. Anyone can do his work, however hard, for one day, Anyone can live sweetly, patiently, lovingly, purely, till the sun goes down. And this is all that life really means."

Another way is to make duty the supreme obligation of life. As Robert E. Lee wrote to his son, Custis Lee: "Duty then is the sublimest word in our language. Do your duty in all things. You cannot do more. You should never wish to do less."

A third way to develop a courageous personality is to realize that the alternative to the impending danger is more dreadful than the danger itself. Elmer Davis had this thought in mind when he said: "Atomic warfare is bad enough; biological warfare would be worse; but there is something that is worse than either . . . . it is subjection to an alien oppressor."

And, finally, the best way for us to develop courageous personalities is to have faith in ourselves, faith in the righteousness of our cause, and faith in the promises of God. This is true because faith is a sure antidote for fear.

If we keep faith and have courage, we can face with confidence the perilous days which lie ahead.

Sam Ervin, Jr., was born on September 27, 1896, in Morganton, North Carolina. He was married to the former Margaret Bruce Bell, June 18, 1924. They have three children: Sam J. Ervin, III, Mrs. Gerald M. Hansler, Mrs. William E. Smith. They also have seven grandchildren.

He is an A.B. graduate, University of North Carolina at Chapel Hill, 1917; and an L.L.B. graduate, Harvard Law School, 1922. He was a trustee at the Morganton Graded schools, 1927-30; University of North Carolina at Chapel Hill, 1932-35, 1945-46; Davidson College, 1948-58.

He is permanent president of the Class of 1917, University of North Carolina at Chapel Hill and was president of General Alumni Association of University of North Carolina at Chapel Hill, 1947-48.

Senator Ervin has been a judge at Burke County Criminal Court; judge on the North Carolina Superior Court; Associate Justice, North Carolina Supreme Court; Representative from Burke County in North Carolina Legislature; Representative from tenth district of North Carolina; and United States Senator from North Carolina since 1954.

Governor J. James Exon of Nebraska

It has been said that men without principles are dangerous, but principles without men are useless. I believe that!

Let me suggest that leaders alone do not make a nation strong. It is the moral fiber of any nation, found rooted in its individual citizens, which determines the heights to which any society can aspire. Certainly this is a time of rapid change, and there is little comfort for those who insist upon being merely spectators. There is much satisfaction, however, for those who choose to participate in a full and meaningful way.

Each one of us knows that every generation writes a page in history. Whether good or bad, that page is indeed recorded. If it is bad, future generations will suffer; if it is good, our children and our grandchildren will welcome their inheritance.

Our nation stands on the threshold of its two-hundredth birthday; this bicentennial celebration will serve as a catalyst for many to reflect on the achievements of the past and our aspirations for the future. Grassroots Americans, and those chosen to positions of leadership, will be making evaluations as to where we are . . . and where we are going.

America is not a perfect nation; certainly we have flaws which only the stupid would deny . . . but more important

than our shortcomings is the fact that America has tradi-
tionally been an idealistic nation! America is a nation
constantly in search of justice. Our record of accomplish-
ment in that regard is the envy of the world. We are blessed.

As with any blessing, there is a balancing responsibility
placed upon each one of us to acknowledge our steward-
ship. America comprises about 6 percent of the world's
population and about 56 percent of the world's wealth!
I am sobered by the biblical quotation that puts this kind
of startling statistic into proper perspective: "Of those to
whom much is given, much is required."

Maturity has turned my attention to the argument that
our success has come largely from a fortunate combination
provided by our Judeo-Christian ethics. As an individual
citizen, and as governor of my state, I firmly believe in
the presence of a public morality as the basis of an orderly
and stable society in America. Our public morality, our
community standards, our value system,—call it what you
will—has been, and is, a precious asset.

Many of us actually witnessed the degeneration of one
of the world's most educated nations under the leadership
of Adolph Hitler. Germany saw its demise because of a
moral collapse; this historical perspective proved to me
that nations cannot survive by intelligence alone. Spiritual
guidelines are required by nations, families, and individuals. Lacking this, even the finest can descend to barbarism.

Moral strength cannot be taken for granted, and no
nation, not even this generation, can go adrift for a decade,
or even a year, without losing its way. Democracy *demands*
a set of values which stretches the moral fiber and challenges our apathy.

I think of the famous quotation which says, "all that is required for the triumph of evil is for good men to do nothing." Dedication to principles improves the lot of mankind, and has through the ages. It seems to me that every age has cried for men who could and would stand up—men, who because of a vision for justice and the courage to be accountable, would see our nation rise to greatness, because we were striving for goodness.

I remind myself that our nation does have a heritage. We have believed that we are our brother's keeper, but in the study of history we submit that we mortals have made less of a success of this world than any had envisioned. We seek success for all mankind with the realization that any of us, even those with official status, have little chance of success in reaching our individual and collective goals unless we can somehow learn and be worthy of guidance from a Supreme Being, whom we have too long ignored.

As a husband, a father, and as governor, I have placed faith and trust in four things: God, family, the moral fiber of this nation, and the ability of one person to make a positive difference.

I believe that the whole issue resolves itself to a final meeting between a man and his Maker. On that day, I pray the Lord will look upon me and say, "Well done, good and faithful servant."

J. James Exon was born in Geddes, South Dakota, August 9, 1921. He attended the University of Omaha. He is married and has one son and two daughters.

Exon served in the United States Army Signal Corps from

1942-45 and in the Army Reserve from 1945 to 1949.

He has been governor of Nebraska since January, 1971. He was a delegate to the Democratic National Convention in 1964; vice-chairman of Nebraska State Democratic Central Committee, 1964 to 1968; Democratic National Committeeman, 1968 to present; member of National Governor's Conference Executive Committee, 1971-72.

He is a thirty-second degree mason; and a past president, Lincoln Optimists Club.

Governor Exon is an Episcopalian.

Governor Wendell Ford of Kentucky

For many years the words "Be still, and know that I am God" (Ps. 46:10) have served as an inspiration and guidance in my everyday living. They offer personal significance to me, because they are a constant reminder that regardless of our wealth or poverty, our success or failure, it is only how God sees us that really matters.

This particular passage also reminds me that life on earth is temporary and that while here, service to God makes our life more meaningful.

I believe that man is placed on earth to do God's will— that of helping others—and I have found that I can best meet this responsibility in government. When considering that government should exist solely to serve people, one can easily understand how God's will can and should be accomplished through governmental affairs. It is not always easy, and I have a favorite prayer which often gives me the additional strength when times appear unusually difficult:

> O LORD
> Give us the strength to accept with serenity
> the things that cannot be changed,
> Give us the courage to change what can and
> should be changed,
> Give us the wisdom to distinguish one from
> the other. Amen.

Wendell H. Ford, Kentucky's forty-ninth governor, was born September 8, 1924, in Daviess County, Kentucky, son of the late state Senator and Mrs. E.M. Ford. A graduate of Daviess County High School in Owensboro, the Governor attended the University of Kentucky and was graduated from the Maryland School of Insurance in 1947.

Governor Ford's introduction to state government came in 1959 when he was chief administrative assistant to Governor Bert Combs. In 1965, he was elected to the state Senate as representative of Daviess and Hancock counties in the Eighth Congressional District. In 1967, he was elected Kentucky's Lieutenant Governor, which served as a stepping stone to his election for a four-year term as Governor in November, 1971.

Governor Ford was married to the former Jean Neel of Owensboro on September 18, 1943. The Fords have two children, a daughter, Mrs. Shirley Dexter of Owensboro, and a son, Steve, who attends the University of Kentucky.

Senator Ernest F. Hollings of South Carolina

Nowadays, all too few of us ever pause to ponder the impact of religion in America. Oh, we can all point out that the quest for religious freedom had a lot to do with the founding of the colonies. And most of us can get off a vague generalization or two about the importance of religion to the development of this great land. But those easy generalizations do justice to neither our religion nor our nation.

Although America has no state religion, it was founded as a religious state. And throughout its history, religion was a vital factor in holding our people together, in instilling a sense of community and of shared experiences. Without that sense of community—that exhilirating sense of togetherness in life's challenges—no people can achieve greatness.

Today the times are much different. We no longer share a real feeling of kinship and brotherhood with one another. Gone is that old spirit of community that bound us together as we struggled to settle a new continent, conquer the mountain barriers, and develop the vast frontier beyond.

Maybe we are too big now and can never reinstill that sense of oneness that makes a people great. Maybe we are too rich and complacent now to respond to the demands of greatness.

Maybe we are just plain tired—weary to the bone—worn out by the fast-paced lives we lead, weary of cold wars and hot wars and all the domestic turmoil we have witnessed, fed up with moving from crisis to crisis with no time out for a rest.

There is a lack of direction, a lack of self-confidence, that becomes each day more dangerous. People everywhere are in flight—fleeing from city to suburb, fleeing from crime and violence, fleeing from mutual tolerance—fleeing, sadly, from one another. We can flee everything except our problems.

A major part of the problem is that we have lost sight of some of our traditional beliefs and commitments. We need to return to our earlier ideals if we are once more to soar into the heights of greatness.

The foremost guiding principle to which we must rededicate ourselves is the Golden Rule. It has the same relevance today as it always had. The world's greatest philosophies, no matter how recondite and esoteric, always boil down to the essence of the Golden Rule.

Another central theme of our rededication should be to appreciate both the individualistic and social aspects of Christianity. Much more needs to be done in ministering to the individual soul. But I would also argue that more concentration on the individual does not preclude similar focus on the social dimensions of Christian life.

Christianity ideally ministers to the *whole man*—to man in all facets of his existence. To ignore one segment is to ignore one facet of man. There is surely no theological reason why Christianity should not make increased dedication to securing orderly and productive change.

No one doubts that our society falls glaringly short of the Christian ideal. Other societies may be even farther from that ideal, but the fact remains that we have much to do. By identifying itself with the necessity for fruitful change, Christianity not only fulfills its own imperatives, but it also helps create an environment wherein the institutions of today can be harnassed to the future instead of being rudely and ignorantly cast aside, as some would do.

In this period of rapid change, religion has no summons more urgent than the encouragement of stability amidst all the inevitable flux. The ground on which we stand shifts so quickly that insecurity runs rampant through the nation. Religion teaches us that this need not be so.

True Christianity accomodates and encourages rational change at the same time that it provides security to the individual person. Change without a spiritual foundation brings only regression and chaos. But change that comes with a continuing faith in God is change for the better.

My faith in God and in the tenets of Christianity are today stronger than ever. My confidence in the future abounds, in spite of the many problems I have outlined herein. I believe America is still at heart a religious nation, and that with some reflection and recommitment, our people—acting on their faith—can enter a new golden age, both for themselves and their neighbors and fellow citizens.

Senator Hollings was born January 1, 1922, in Charleston, South Carolina. He is married to Rita Liddy and they have four children: Michael Milhous, Helen Hayne, Patricia Salley, and Ernest Frederick, III.

He was educated in the Charleston public schools; he received an A.B. degree from The Citadel in 1942 and a L.L.D. degree from the University of South Carolina Law School in 1947. Senator Hollings has been a member and a past president of the Law Federation; a member of South Carolina Law Review and of the Wig and Robe Honor Society; and was president of the alumni of The Citadel in 1954. He received the L.L.D. degree from The Citadel in 1959 and the Doctor of Laws from Benedict College in 1971.

Hollings is a member of the Lutheran church; he served on the Lutheran Church of America Executive Council from 1962 to 1968 and on the Court of Adjudication, Lutheran Church.

Senator Hollings has been involved in the following aspects of public service: South Carolina House of Representatives, 1948, Speaker Pro-Tem, 1951-53; lieutenant governor of South Carolina, 1955 to 1959; governor of South Carolina, 1959 to 1963. He was elected to the United States Senate in 1966 and was reelected to a full term in 1968.

Clarence M. Kelley, Director, Federal Bureau of Investigation

I have been in public life for thirty-three years. Twenty-one years of this period have been with the FBI, and twelve with the Kansas City, Missouri, Police Department. During my tenure with the FBI, I served as Agent, then in numerous supervisory positions, and now hold the position of Director. Twelve years were spent as Chief of Police at Kansas City, Missouri.

On numerous occasions during this career I have seen the need for faith, whether it be faith in yourself, a principle, or religious faith. I think perhaps the maximum position to be attained by any official who has responsibilities is that he have all three of these. The strongest of all undeniably is faith that stems from a strong religious belief. When this is established, the other two fall in line as a natural consequence of the first.

In the role of a decision maker, and particularly in the field of law enforcement, we have many difficult and perplexing decisions. Without doubt there is no area where life and death questions present themselves so keenly unless it is in the military. There is also no area wherein the limelight of publicity shines so brightly and brings out so vividly the questions of judgment as to what is right and what is wrong.

Many of these decisions must be made without the benefit of great reflection and review of all causation factors. In other words, the decision maker must depend on an intuitive sense of good judgment and a pattern of life and belief which enable him to make the right decision.

I, therefore, am firmly of the conviction that if a public official cast in this role does not have the capability of calling upon the three sources of faith to aid him in his decision, he cannot perform properly with the maximum effectiveness. It can almost be said without equivocation that the faith in the religion actually not only fortifies the other two, but gives direction insofar as their exercise.

I have been a member of the Christian Church during practically all of my life. This afforded me a broad base of proper ethics, which in essence is synonymous with Christian philosophy.

It becomes a matter of course when the official must make a decision that he call upon his past experiences. When those experiences are steeped in understanding from a knowledge of what is right and what is good, and if his faith is strong enough, he will almost automatically be brought to the right decision.

Obviously there are going to be some occasions when he will make an error in judgment, but this is not because of a false base for his decision making, but usually because of an erroneous appraisal of that base. Were all of us to be guided by solid Christian principles, seldom would we err.

In this atmosphere of awesome decisions it is indeed comforting to have as a backdrop the lessons of faith. I am thankful that I can enjoy the luxury of this assistance.

Mr. Kelley was born October 24, 1911, in Kansas City, Missouri. He received a B.A. degree from the University of Kansas and an L.L.B. degree from the University of Kansas City, Missouri.

Mr. Kelley entered on duty with the FBI as a Special Agent on October 7, 1940. Based on his outstanding ability and performance, he was assigned supervisory duties at FBI Headquarters in 1951. During July, 1953, he was transferred to the Houston Office where he served as Assistant Special Agent in Charge until July, 1955. Mr. Kelley was transferred to the Training and Inspection Division at FBI Headquarters and shortly thereafter was designated Inspector.

Kelley became Chief of Police at Kansas City, Missouri, after his retirement from the FBI in 1961. This was the position he was holding at the time of his nomination for Director of the FBI.

Kelley and his wife, Ruby, have a son and a married daughter, both of whom reside in Kansas City.

Governor Bruce King of New Mexico

I am a Christian.

I can honestly and truthfully make that statement from the standpoint of my religious conviction; and I can truthfully say that I try to practice my Christian beliefs in my daily relationships with my fellowman, both in my public and my private life.

Being a Christian in public life involves special concerns and considerations, I think. Obviously, not all of those with whom a public official must deal believe or practice the same Christian ethic, and this can cause some consternation. But one cannot be a Christian only with Christians, and something different for others.

In the larger sense, of course, a true practicing Christian is not really unnerved by special concerns or considerations, because he does not need to consciously change his manner of functioning according to a particular situation. His faith should not only be apparent from his actions, but it should give him the confidence to do the right thing regardless of the possible consequences.

His faith should convince him of the presence of a Higher Power and a Stronger Hand in the affairs of men, such that even if he seems not to succeed in his own strong position he can see even his failure as a part of the larger plan. I have found so often that courses of action which seem destined to lead us to bad consequences have a way of changing directions and ending up where they should be, and so I continue to have confidence that God still rules the world and that he uses us mortal men—public servants—to accomplish the ends he himself has appointed. Secure in this faith I am able to go about my daily tasks knowing that my decisions, when prayerfully considered, are led in the right direction.

In these days of uncertainty for this great nation, when shortages plague us, when friends desert us, when public confidence in our political system and elected officials has so badly eroded, we need to turn to some strong fountain of support.

A person of faith knows where to turn, and will find himself replenished and refreshed at the divine fountain of grace. As a rancher, I constantly see the miracle of birth and life and renewal, and it is hard for me to understand how others, seeing these same things, cannot accept the presence of divine guidance in the affairs of men.

For years I have taught a Sunday School class of young people and it is an inspiring thing to witness young lives—some of whom may themselves become public servants—in the formulation of their beliefs and the directions which will hopefully influence them throughout their futures. If we are successful in this early training, we should have some degree of assurance in the future security of our nation and of our world.

It would be easy to list here the tenets of faith in which I believe; or to enumerate those principles to which I hold. But I am certain that those who read these words would say: "Big deal; what is so different about what he believes?

It's the same old thing!"

But isn't that really a part of the fabric of faith—the constancy, the permanence, the fact that so many others for so long have subscribed to these same tenets that have withstood the test of time and the adversity of persecution? My faith is a positive thing, not a series of negatives. God *is,* and for me and for all who believe, he is a positive influence on the road which leads to life eternal. That, very simply, is a statement of my belief.

In the words of Thomas Jefferson, "When a man assumes a public trust, he should consider himself public property." And as Abraham Lincoln said in his Second Inaugural Address, "With malice toward none; with charity for all; with firmness in the right, as God gives us to see the right, let us strive on to finish the work we are in."

Bruce King was elected Governor of New Mexico November 3, 1970, and took office January 1, 1971, as the twenty-first man to serve as New Mexico's chief executive since statehood in 1912.

A native New Mexican, Governor King was born April 6, 1924, near Stanley on the family homestead, the third of four children born to Mr. and Mrs. William King. He attended the University of New Mexico. He is married to the former Alice Marie Martin of Moriarty. They have two sons, Bill and Gary.

After serving the United States Army Field Artillery in the South Pacific during World War II, he returned to New Mexico to devote himself, with his brothers, to expanding the family ranching operations, which now include three ranches in six counties.

He first held public office from 1955-58 as Santa Fe County Commissioner and was Chairman in 1957-58. He then served ten years as southern Santa Fe County's delegate to the New Mexico House of Representatives, and served as Speaker from 1963 to 1968. His six years as Speaker of the House stand as a record for that office. In 1969, he was elected president of the New Mexico Constitutional Convention.

He has served as Governor of New Mexico since January, 1971, the first Governor in recent history to serve a four-year term. His memberships include the New Mexico Farm and Livestock Bureau, New Mexico Cattle Growers Association, American Cattle Growers, New Mexico Soil and Water Conservation Commission, the Elks, and the American Legion.

Governor Richard Kneip of South Dakota

I am very pleased to have this opportunity to offer a statement of my personal faith. This is a time when many people doubt their beliefs and the integrity and morality of other people's actions. The philosophy of "anything goes" is very prevalent. This atmosphere of doubt and confusion makes it even more important that we offer testimony to the important role faith can play.

My faith in God has been a vital, motivating factor in my life. I do not look upon a life of faith as a passive observance of a belief. The mass, the sacraments, and prayer are necessary expressions of faith, and they are very important to me, but what I do because of my faith is equally important. Faith gives me a purpose in life. Christ expressed that purpose when he said, "Thou shalt love thy neighbour as thyself" (Matt. 22:39).

We live in a world in which a majority of our "neighbours" go to bed hungry every night. It is a world in which many more people live daily with poverty, poor health, lack of education, and hunger than experience color television, automatic dishwashers, and the other amenities of life that some of us have grown accustomed to.

Christ's commandment to love our neighbors means more to me than just contributing to the collection plate on Sunday morning. It means that I must follow his exam-

ple by becoming actively involved in efforts to meet the social and economic and spiritual needs of my fellowman.

Many people are critical of government today. They see it as an immoral, impersonal vice pressing in on them. I see it in a different light. I became involved in government because of its capacity to help people. It is one way I can practice my belief that an individual who accepts the teachings of Christ must become involved.

Individual human beings have a God-given capacity to grow and think and learn and create. This capacity is severely limited when they are denied the basic economic and social necessities. Government's role should be to see that these basic necessities are provided. It should be an active tool for social justice.

My involvement in government has been based on this concept of the role government can play in enhancing the quality of human life. I have worked for comprehensive tax reform in my state because I believe the present one places an unjust burden on those least able to pay.

I have worked to reorganize state government so that it will be more capable of delivering services to the people. I have opposed capital punishment, abortion on demand, and undeclared warfare because I believe these things are inimical to the goal of improving the quality of life for all human beings.

Obviously, government is not the only area which needs the involvement of people motivated by high standards of Christian concern for their fellowman. It happens to be my area of involvement, and therefore I am especially concerned that people be aware of the important role government can play. Whether as a scientist, engineer, farmer, teacher, businessman, or in any other profession, an individual can contribute if he is just willing to live his faith. The important thing to remember is that Christian beliefs are static if they are not put to use in daily life.

Many young people have become disillusioned about Christianity because they see the church as being more involved in budgets and capital improvements than in serving the needs of people. This is something only the members of the church can change, and they do it by accepting their social responsibilities.

The type of concern I have been referring to is that which is directed outward, beyond our personal family relationships. It is equally important to live faith within the family. The old saying that children learn more from action than from words is very true. It is important to teach children about values and ideals, to believe in God and the church, and to be actively concerned about the welfare of people. It is even more important that the parents live the kind of lives that indicate they believe in these things also.

Family life is very important to me. Although my duties as governor demand a lot of my time, I spend as much time as possible with my family. I have always believed it is in the home that children learn to value the vital role Christian faith can play in their lives. If there is one thing I hope to pass on to my children, it is this.

Admittedly, I have placed a lot of emphasis in this statement on what I call "Christianity in action." I do not mean to slight the role faith plays in the individual's life at all. Certainly it has given meaning and purpose to my life.

I feel very sorry for people who are unable to accept the idea that there is a God and that they do have the opportunity to spend eternal life in heaven. For many years the popular belief has seemed to be that all of reality can be quantified, and that which is incapable of being quantified does not exist—therefore, God cannot exist. Fortunately, we are experiencing a rebirth of the realization that there is much more to life than this viewpoint permits. Hopefully more and more people will come to realize that *belief in God does make a difference.*

For myself, I can say that my Christian faith is vital to me, not only in terms of my own eternal life, but also in terms of my commitment to serving my fellowman. "Love thy neighbour as thyself" is a commandment that I do not take lightly.

The work Governor Kneip is doing includes reorganization of the executive branch of state government, the establishment of sub-state planning and development districts under the Rural Model Development Program, and emphasis on natural resource conservation and environment protection.

Governor Kneip's recent honors include appointment by President Richard M. Nixon to the Advisory Commission of Intergovernmental Relations and election to the Executive Committee of the National Governors' Conference (1972-1973).

erience during World War II included fi
ns on a B-24. Wounded over Vienna, Austr
d the Purple Heart. He also earned the A
Oak Leaf Clusters and the European Ribb
le stars.

he former Helen Wallbank of Denver, Co
e two children, Bill, Jr., of Colorado Sprin
Elaine, a graduate of Smith College, w
w degree at the University of Michigan.

Governor William G. Milliken of Michigan

I can't say how history will finally judge this past year, but one thing is certain: it was a year of great consequences.

In a year such as we have just passed through, one gets the impression that the whole system is crumbling before our eyes—the political system, the social system, the system of values, and finally, considering what is happening to the dollar, the economic system.

What remains for us to believe in in an age when the forces of change seem more powerful than man's ability to assimilate change? Despite what the cynics say, and the cynics seem to have the upper hand at the moment, I believe there is a *great deal that Americans can believe in.*

Millions of Americans still believe in God, and the quest for religious meaning that so many young people have embarked on is especially heartening.

Millions of Americans still believe in this country, still believe that the visions of the founders lie well within the boundaries of the possible, and that one day those visions will become reality.

Millions of Americans believe that the earth is worth preserving, that space is worth exploring, that a good education is worth struggling for, that the last vestiges of racism should be eliminated, that our prosperity should be shared by everyone.

The fact is that millions of Americans still have faith in a variety of things, and that no combination of events, no collection of dire prophecies, can shatter those enduring faiths.

You have your faiths, and I have mine. Perhaps the most important faith we can have together is faith in people—faith in each other. For there is, I believe, no evil that people cannot overcome, no social ill that people cannot cure, no political fault that people cannot correct.

One thinks of the terrible harm that the Nazis inflicted in World War II, and their final destruction at the hands of millions of ordinary people who fought to preserve principles of decency and freedom. One thinks how millions of black people lived through the agonies of slavery until an aroused nation went to war to free them.

One thinks of courage of countless individuals against odds that seemed insurmountable; one thinks of the patient suffering of the Vietnam prisoners who were finally released.

In his speech accepting the Nobel Prize for Literature in 1960, William Faulkner has this to say:

I decline to accept the end of man. It is easy enough to say that man is immortal simply because he will endure; that when the last ding-dong of doom has clanged and faded from the last worthless rock hanging tideless in the last red and dying evening, that even then there will still be one more sound: that of his puny inexhaustible voice, still talking.

I refuse to accept this. I believe that man will not merely endure: he will prevail. He is immortal, not because he alone among creatures has an inexhaustible voice, but because he has

---

a soul, a spirit capable of c
ance.

That is what we must b
spirit, man's compassion
care, I believe they will
injustice and reducing th

Michigan's governor,
background as lieutenan
executive, and civic lead
verse City on March 2(
governor in 1964 and re
four years in the State
he was Majority Floor L
uary 22, 1969, when (
United States Secretary (
Governor Milliken then
November, 1970.
Governor Milliken, (
received honorary Docto
of Michigan, Eastern M
University, Western M
Institute of Technology.
Letters degree from N(
He is a member of
College in Northampto(
as a trustee of Northw(
to 1955, he was a m
Commission.

Combat ex
combat missi(
he was awar(
Medal with tw
with three ba(
His wife is
rado. They ha
Colorado, an(
is pursuing a

Senator John O. Pastore of Rhode Island

To be invited to contribute to the topics "Politics and Religion Can Mix," I am inclined to suggest that the theme should be "Politics and Religion Must Mix!"

Speaking from the viewpoint of my office, that of United States Senator, a senator's life is inseparable from that of his constituents. He is privileged to share their most intimate problems—their fears and their failures—their triumphs and their troubles—their worries and their wants.

The senator often experiences the frankness with which a man or woman confides in their confessor. A senator knows there must be a code of conduct between persons to protect the weak and restrain the overbearing.

Society must have such standards to promote the security and serenity of its members. Our government is a society which interprets security and serenity as "life, liberty and the pursuit of happiness."

It was founded in the belief that equality of birth and opportunity are the gifts of God. This is the God whom our founding fathers acknowledged. This is the God who, speaking to man in time, gave us the Ten Commandements as the guide to the individual and common good—for man's temporal well-being and eternal happiness.

By fortune of birth I am a Christian, accepting the divinty of a documented figure of history, Christ, who called himself the Son of God and permitted others so to call him—

proved his divinity by miracles—fed the hungry—healed the sick—and reaffirmed the test of the Ten Commandments.

I acknowledge them for myself personally and accept them as the standards of government pledged "to promote the general welfare and secure the blessings of liberty."

Politics is the art of directing the interplay of the functions of government—legislative, executive and judicial—to secure for its citizens the material and spiritual values of creation—of nature, the arts and sciences—culture and concern for human well-being. Politics must be based on the tenets of religion which is man's and government's relation to God.

Politics has a responsibility for moral leadership to give a sense of direction to a people divided and doubtful as they are assailed by the social and economic perils of the day.

A modern authority—a clergyman steeped in the human problems of our greatest city—declares that our approach to moral leadership must be universal if we are to help the individual make the complex moral decisions required of him.

This modern authority urges that our approach to moral leadership must be universal. "There are situations in society," he says, "that demand not new laws, but dispassionate attention of whole communities. Has our society been focusing its attention sufficiently on its most fundamental moral issues—economic exploitation, inequality of opportunity, political and military accountability, adequate evaluation of schools, wars and production of war machines instead of more beneficial products, personal irresponsibility in some life-styles, a just immigration policy, use of wholesale abortions instead of finding effective means of birth control, racism, escapism through drugs, our worldwide responsibility to the poor?"

That authority is a distinguished clergyman. Religion *can* and *must mix* with the obligations of politics. Politics and religion must mix.

In passing I have mentioned man's "eternal happiness." As an article of my faith I accept Christ's promise of the resurrection of the body. I cannot conceive that all the beauties of creation—all the loveliness of man's relation to his Creator—should disappear in the oblivion of nothingness.

United States Senator John O. Pastore was born in Providence, Rhode Island, March 17, 1907.

He received the Bachelor of Laws degree from Northeastern University in 1931.

Senator Pastore has served in the following capacities: Rhode Island General Assembly, 1935; assistant attorney general, 1937-38, 1940-44; lieutenant governor, 1944-45; governor, 1945-50; United States Senator from December 18, 1950.

He has served on the following Senate committee assignments: Appropriations, Joint Committee on Atomic Energy, Senate Commerce Committee, Senate Democratic Policy Committee.

Senator Pastore married Elena Elizabeth Caito in 1941. They have three children: John O. Pastore, Jr., M.D.; Mrs. Frances Scheuer, wife of Alfred Q. Scheuer, M.D.; and Louise Marie Harbourt, B.S., R.N., wife of Clifford M. Harbourt.

Senator Jennings Randolph of West Virginia

Although we all are men and women in our own capacities, we are but children of God. And so I am never completely lost amidst the perplexities of politics and pressures and contesting powers. Faith is within me. I marvel at the astronauts in outer space, but I realize that we need the inner peace to use fully such achievements to benefit mankind.

The most fundamental resource of this nation is its spiritual strength. Our country needs now the witnessing of a rebirth of individual and collective responsibility. We also need a profession of faith in ourselves, not only in our religion, but in our democratic government and its people. Our lives are often characterized by a sense of doubt and by disagreement on the directions in which our nation should proceed in the 70's.

I confess to anxiety, if not alarm, over what I see as a general softening of the Protestant ethic. The action of the individual Christian contributes to the action of the whole. If we are lackadaisical in support of our religious convictions, then the overall effectiveness of the church will be hampered. An enlightened and dedicated membership is needed, alert to the opportunities for service in their support of the denomination or faith they profess.

Our differences need not be divisive. It's when we are indifferent to our pressing problems that we need to awaken and to act. We need to learn to speak strongly our convictions, but we can do so without the cutting words that wound. I pray for that day, not fixed on the calendar, when we will be able to live together as neighbors. We must find a basis for mutual respect of different nationalities. We must break the barriers of misunderstanding. We must ultimately travel a common pathway to peace.

I am a realist yet a sentimentalist. When night falls, assessment of the day comes. We who run so fast often fail to read and heed.

Ten years ago I lay flat on my back after an operation for a detached retina. My eyes were completely covered with black patches. My body was made immobile by sandbags to prevent the slightest movement. The surgeon told me frankly before the operation, "There is a chance that you may be blind in one eye."

Many thoughts raced through my mind. I considered my role as a man, as a husband, as a father, as a public servant, and as a Christian. Meditation during those quiet and dark days and nights further strengthened my faith. Also, because of that experience I can better understand, as chairman of the Subcommittee on the Handicapped, the continuous darkness that faces blind Americans.

I was reared in a religious home. Prayer was a part of my homelife. As a young child in Salem, West Virginia, I remember vividly my grandfather offering prayers at mealtime.

When I was graduated from college, my mother's gift to me was a Bible, which I continue to read and cherish. In the flyleaf she had carefully written, in her penned script, words so simple yet so meaningful: "Each for the other, and both for God."

Mrs. Randoph and I are happy that our sons continue in their religious beliefs. I see the effects of worship on my grandchildren, and how God helps fit all of life together.

My wife and I know that prayers are helpful. The opportunity for prayer is one of God's greatest gifts. I am an advocate of permitting voluntary prayers in public buildings, including schools.

Various studies have shown that we fast-moving Americans fear silence. Yet we need silence. Job 23:3 states, "Oh that I knew where I might find him." We need silence to let God talk to us and guide us—to discuss with him personal problems and burdens of the day which seem large, but in many instances are small in comparison with problems that are facing others.

I am thankful for my spiritual upbringing and its influence on my public career. When I entered politics more than four decades ago, a wise newspaper editor told me that the only "safe" issues to speak about were God and country. Yet I find, among some groups, that these are two of the most controversial issues.

The finest lesson an individual can learn before complete awareness and acceptance of God and his divine order, is that human limitations are set by divine law, not by the individual. Without order, freedom becomes chaos.

From the beginning, thinking men and women have recognized that a society without the structure of authority to command respect and maintain justice and order is a society doomed to collapse. To exist as a family, as a group, as a nation, we must live within a framework of limitations words so simple yet so meaningful: "Each for the other, and both for God."

Mrs. Randoph and I are happy that our sons continue in their religious beliefs. I see the effects of worship on my grandchildren, and how God helps fit all of life together.

My wife and I know that prayers are helpful. The opportunity for prayer is one of God's greatest gifts. I am an advocate of permitting voluntary prayers in public buildings, including schools.

Various studies have shown that we fast-moving Americans fear silence. Yet we need silence. Job 23:3 states, "Oh that I knew where I might find him." We need silence to let God talk to us and guide us—to discuss with him personal problems and burdens of the day which seem large, but in many instances are small in comparison with problems that are facing others.

I am thankful for my spiritual upbringing and its influence on my public career. When I entered politics more than four decades ago, a wise newspaper editor told me that the only "safe" issues to speak about were God and country. Yet I find, among some groups, that these are two of the most controversial issues.

The finest lesson an individual can learn before complete awareness and acceptance of God and his divine order, is that human limitations are set by divine law, not by the individual. Without order, freedom becomes chaos.

From the beginning, thinking men and women have recognized that a society without the structure of authority to command respect and maintain justice and order is a society doomed to collapse. To exist as a family, as a group, as a nation, we must live within a framework of limitations

Our differences need not be divisive. It's when we are indifferent to our pressing problems that we need to awaken and to act. We need to learn to speak strongly our convictions, but we can do so without the cutting words that wound. I pray for that day, not fixed on the calendar, when we will be able to live together as neighbors. We must find a basis for mutual respect of different nationalities. We must break the barriers of misunderstanding. We must ultimately travel a common pathway to peace.

I am a realist yet a sentimentalist. When night falls, assessment of the day comes. We who run so fast often fail to read and heed.

Ten years ago I lay flat on my back after an operation for a detached retina. My eyes were completely covered with black patches. My body was made immobile by sandbags to prevent the slightest movement. The surgeon told me frankly before the operation, "There is a chance that you may be blind in one eye."

Many thoughts raced through my mind. I considered my role as a man, as a husband, as a father, as a public servant, and as a Christian. Meditation during those quiet and dark days and nights further strengthened my faith. Also, because of that experience I can better understand, as chairman of the Subcommittee on the Handicapped, the continuous darkness that faces blind Americans.

I was reared in a religious home. Prayer was a part of my homelife. As a young child in Salem, West Virginia, I remember vividly my grandfather offering prayers at mealtime.

When I was graduated from college, my mother's gift to me was a Bible, which I continue to read and cherish. In the flyleaf she had carefully written, in her penned script,

Governor William G. Milliken of Michigan

I can't say how history will finally judge this past year, but one thing is certain: it was a year of great consequences.

In a year such as we have just passed through, one gets the impression that the whole system is crumbling before our eyes—the political system, the social system, the system of values, and finally, considering what is happening to the dollar, the economic system.

What remains for us to believe in in an age when the forces of change seem more powerful than man's ability to assimilate change? Despite what the cynics say, and the cynics seem to have the upper hand at the moment, I believe there is a *great deal that Americans can believe in.*

Millions of Americans still believe in God, and the quest for religious meaning that so many young people have embarked on is especially heartening.

Millions of Americans still believe in this country, still believe that the visions of the founders lie well within the boundaries of the possible, and that one day those visions will become reality.

Millions of Americans believe that the earth is worth preserving, that space is worth exploring, that a good education is worth struggling for, that the last vestiges of racism should be eliminated, that our prosperity should be shared by everyone.

The fact is that millions of Americans still have faith in a variety of things, and that no combination of events, no collection of dire prophecies, can shatter those enduring faiths.

You have your faiths, and I have mine. Perhaps the most important faith we can have together is faith in people—faith in each other. For there is, I believe, no evil that people cannot overcome, no social ill that people cannot cure, no political fault that people cannot correct.

One thinks of the terrible harm that the Nazis inflicted in World War II, and their final destruction at the hands of millions of ordinary people who fought to preserve principles of decency and freedom. One thinks how millions of black people lived through the agonies of slavery until an aroused nation went to war to free them.

One thinks of courage of countless individuals against odds that seemed insurmountable; one thinks of the patient suffering of the Vietnam prisoners who were finally released.

In his speech accepting the Nobel Prize for Literature in 1960, William Faulkner has this to say:

I decline to accept the end of man. It is easy enough to say that man is immortal simply because he will endure; that when the last ding-dong of doom has clanged and faded from the last worthless rock hanging tideless in the last red and dying evening, that even then there will still be one more sound: that of his puny inexhaustible voice, still talking.

I refuse to accept this. I believe that man will not merely endure: he will prevail. He is immortal, not because he alone among creatures has an inexhaustible voice, but because he has a soul, a spirit capable of compassion and sacrifice and endurance.

That is what we must believe in today: man's soul, man's spirit, man's compassion. And because men and women care, I believe they will prevail, defeating evil, correcting injustice and reducing the burdens of the unfortunate.

Michigan's governor, William G. Milliken, has a varied background as lieutenant governor, state senator, business executive, and civic leader. The Governor was born in Traverse City on March 26, 1922. He was elected lieutenant governor in 1964 and reelected in 1966, after having served four years in the State Senate, the last two years of which he was Majority Floor Leader. He became governor on January 22, 1969, when Governor George Romney became United States Secretary of Housing and Urban Development. Governor Milliken then was elected to a four-year term in November, 1970.

Governor Milliken, a graduate of Yale University, has received honorary Doctor of Law degrees from the University of Michigan, Eastern Michigan University, Central Michigan University, Western Michigan University, and the Detroit Institute of Technology. He has honorary Doctor of Humane Letters degree from Northern Michigan University.

He is a member of the Board of Counselors of Smith College in Northampton University, and served for three years as a trustee of Northwestern Michigan College. From 1947 to 1955, he was a member of the Michigan Waterways Commission.

Combat experience during World War II included fifty combat missions on a B-24. Wounded over Vienna, Austria, he was awarded the Purple Heart. He also earned the Air Medal with two Oak Leaf Clusters and the European Ribbon with three battle stars.

His wife is the former Helen Wallbank of Denver, Colorado. They have two children, Bill, Jr., of Colorado Springs, Colorado, and Elaine, a graduate of Smith College, who is pursuing a law degree at the University of Michigan.

Senator Jennings Randolph of West Virginia

Although we all are men and women in our own capacities, we are but children of God. And so I am never completely lost amidst the perplexities of politics and pressures and contesting powers. Faith is within me. I marvel at the astronauts in outer space, but I realize that we need the inner peace to use fully such achievements to benefit mankind.

The most fundamental resource of this nation is its spiritual strength. Our country needs now the witnessing of a rebirth of individual and collective responsibility. We also need a profession of faith in ourselves, not only in our religion, but in our democratic government and its people. Our lives are often characterized by a sense of doubt and by disagreement on the directions in which our nation should proceed in the 70's.

I confess to anxiety, if not alarm, over what I see as a general softening of the Protestant ethic. The action of the individual Christian contributes to the action of the whole. If we are lackadaisical in support of our religious convictions, then the overall effectiveness of the church will be hampered. An enlightened and dedicated membership is needed, alert to the opportunities for service in their support of the denomination or faith they profess.

icy, use of wholesale abortions instead of finding effective means of birth control, racism, escapism through drugs, our worldwide responsibility to the poor?"

That authority is a distinguished clergyman. Religion *can* and *must mix* with the obligations of politics. Politics and religion must mix.

In passing I have mentioned man's "eternal happiness." As an article of my faith I accept Christ's promise of the resurrection of the body. I cannot conceive that all the beauties of creation—all the loveliness of man's relation to his Creator—should disappear in the oblivion of nothingness.

United States Senator John O. Pastore was born in Providence, Rhode Island, March 17, 1907.

He received the Bachelor of Laws degree from Northeastern University in 1931.

Senator Pastore has served in the following capacities: Rhode Island General Assembly, 1935; assistant attorney general, 1937-38, 1940-44; lieutenant governor, 1944-45; governor, 1945-50; United States Senator from December 18, 1950.

He has served on the following Senate committee assignments: Appropriations, Joint Committee on Atomic Energy, Senate Commerce Committee, Senate Democratic Policy Committee.

Senator Pastore married Elena Elizabeth Caito in 1941. They have three children: John O. Pastore, Jr., M.D.; Mrs. Frances Scheuer, wife of Alfred Q. Scheuer, M.D.; and Louise Marie Harbourt, B.S., R.N., wife of Clifford M. Harbourt.

proved his divinity by miracles—fed the hungry—healed the sick—and reaffirmed the test of the Ten Commandments.

I acknowledge them for myself personally and accept them as the standards of government pledged "to promote the general welfare and secure the blessings of liberty."

Politics is the art of directing the interplay of the functions of government—legislative, executive and judicial—to secure for its citizens the material and spiritual values of creation—of nature, the arts and sciences—culture and concern for human well-being. Politics must be based on the tenets of religion which is man's and government's relation to God.

Politics has a responsibility for moral leadership to give a sense of direction to a people divided and doubtful as they are assailed by the social and economic perils of the day.

A modern authority—a clergyman steeped in the human problems of our greatest city—declares that our approach to moral leadership must be universal if we are to help the individual make the complex moral decisions required of him.

This modern authority urges that our approach to moral leadership must be universal. "There are situations in society," he says, "that demand not new laws, but dispassionate attention of whole communities. Has our society been focusing its attention sufficiently on its most fundamental moral issues—economic exploitation, inequality of opportunity, political and military accountability, adequate evaluation of schools, wars and production of war machines instead of more beneficial products, personal irresponsibility in some life-styles, a just immigration pol-

Senator John O. Pastore of Rhode Island

To be invited to contribute to the topics "Politics and Religion Can Mix," I am inclined to suggest that the theme should be "Politics and Religion Must Mix!"

Speaking from the viewpoint of my office, that of United States Senator, a senator's life is inseparable from that of his constituents. He is privileged to share their most intimate problems—their fears and their failures—their triumphs and their troubles—their worries and their wants.

The senator often experiences the frankness with which a man or woman confides in their confessor. A senator knows there must be a code of conduct between persons to protect the weak and restrain the overbearing.

Society must have such standards to promote the security and serenity of its members. Our government is a society which interprets security and serenity as "life, liberty and the pursuit of happiness."

It was founded in the belief that equality of birth and opportunity are the gifts of God. This is the God whom our founding fathers acknowledged. This is the God who, speaking to man in time, gave us the Ten Commandements as the guide to the individual and common good—for man's temporal well-being and eternal happiness.

By fortune of birth I am a Christian, accepting the divinty of a documented figure of history, Christ, who called himself the Son of God and permitted others so to call him—

where each individual must work with others for his community. Thus, he provides value as a citizen, and widens his circumference of living. What is needed is redemption—redemption through faith in the law of God and reason.

In our rebirth of responsibility we must pursue peaceably to reconcile the differences between the haves and the have-nots, between the minorities and the majority, between the as-yet unestablished and the so-called 'establishment.' American Christians seem to forget that the very name, Protestant, implies dissent—dissent in social, economic, political, and religious doctrines. Sometimes our differences are really our strengths.

Most members of the United States Congress have personally indicated their religious affiliations or preferences. I am an active member in the Senate Prayer Breakfast Group that meets weekly in the Capitol.

This is the best day of the week for me. It gives me a lift. Members speak on any topic they wish, either a religious subject or one having religious overtones affecting their work and life. We open to each other our errors, our failures, and our faith.

At the end of the session, when we join our hands in prayer, I can feel the grips tightening. We sense that we are going out strengthened. This helps in personal understanding one to the other as we discuss issues in the Senate facing our country and the world.

I am an active Seventh Day Baptist. Saturday is our day of worship and is the basic tenet that makes us different from the other Baptists. After six days of working, the body and mind become tired and on the sabbath we rest in one way or another that we may begin the new week with renewed strength.

The ecumenical movement must learn to understand religions and faiths. The strength of Christ on earth was that he loved all people, and not that he approved of all they did. He loved those who walked with him along the shores of the Sea of Galilee. He loved those who walked with him in the hills, where his cross was hung. He loved all those people along the sea and those in the valley.

We are often weary with all these crosscurrents that blow. Some are evil winds. They bend us. At other times there comes a reassuring tranquility which is of the spirit. To possess it is so rewarding, to deny it or to be denied it is so barren.

Today's church must be active. I believe in separation of church and state but there are public programs which can express humanitarian concern: housing projects, inner-city counseling, rehabilitation work with the handicapped, visiting the elderly. This is true Christian social action—action by which a church expresses concern and does what religion teaches us to do, to help those in need. We church members must go beyond the walls of the church structure to help the less fortunate.

Pastures are not always green and the waters will not always be still. But when the storm beats loudest and I cry out for help, God whispers, "It is I." Yes, where he leads me, I can safely go.

Each day can be a New Day—not just another day. Each day can be the best day of the year.

The spirit shall be nurtured for the tomorrows. We will be needing this spirit more and more if our country is to stand strong and to conquer this era of misdeeds and divisiveness so prevalent.

Jennings Randolph, Democrat, of Elkins, Randolph County, West Virginia, is a United States Senator. He was born at Salem, West Virginia, March 8, 1902. He graduated from Salem Academy in 1920 and from Salem College, magna cum laude, 1924.

Randolph was married in 1933 to Mary Katherine Babb of Keyser, West Virginia. They have two sons, Jennings, Jr., St. Louis, Missouri, and Frank, Washington, D.C. He is a member of Washington Seventh Day Baptist Church and a former Vice-Chairman of the North American Fellowship of the Baptist World Alliance.

Senator Randolph is a former newspaper editor and owner and was professor of public speaking and journalism and director of athletics at Davis and Elkins College from 1927 to 1932. He was assistant to the president and director of public relations, Capital Airlines, 1947 to 1958. He is the author of Going to Make a Speech? *and coauthor of* Mr. Chairman, Ladies and Gentlemen.

Randolph was elected to the United States House of Representatives in 1932 and served from 1933 to 1947. During this time he was assistant majority whip. Elected to United States Senate in November, 1958, to complete the term of Senator M. M. Neely until January, 1961, he was reelected in 1960, 1966, and 1972. His committee assignments have included chairman of Public Works Committee; chairman of Subcommittee on the Handicapped; member of the committees on Labor and Public Welfare, Post Office and Civil Service, and Veterans' Affairs.

Senator Randolph received the Migel Medal from the American Foundation for the Blind, 1972.

Nelson A. Rockefeller of New York

Every public leader must have a philosophic base, a set of principles to steer by as he is called upon to render judgments on the many often-conflicting issues which confront him daily.

My own philosophic base has its roots in the early family influence which shaped and guided me, the Christian teaching of both of my parents, which permeate even my earliest recollections.

Never will I forget my mother's letters to me while I was a boy away at camp or later at college, letters filled—without preaching—with her gentle philosophy which guided us always toward the true brotherhood of man and continually imbued us with a sense of our Christian responsibility toward others.

My father, too, not only shaped the course of his life by Christian principles but also, in his day-to-day contacts with us, passed those traditions on to his children. He taught a men's Bible class at the old Fifth Avenue Baptist Church, but his teaching did not stop there. It was with us every day, from the moment we arose and had family prayers before breakfast until we went to bed at night.

With such a background, it is natural that, even before I first entered public life, I recognized politics not as an end, but a means to an end; that we must be guided by God's admonition that each of us is, indeed, his brother's keeper, and that we must put our belief to work through our public and political actions. Our religious principles must provide an unswerving moral base for our leadership, or that leadership will fail.

I have tried to make those principles the basis of my leadership as the governor of New York. They guided me in my decisions to broaden educational opportunities for all our young people—from the highest per capita support of primary and secondary education in the country to development of the largest state university in the world.

They guided me in my fight to rescue our young people from the soul-destroying synthetic god of drugs. They guided me in the decisions to pioneer the nation's first total program to rescue our waters from pollution, to broaden and strengthen the nation's first State Commission for Human Rights, to create the first State Council on the Arts.

These same convictions about human equality and the worth of the individual have prompted my actions to remove any barriers of race, religion, and sex in employment opportunities, to insure that health care is available to all, to help relieve the burdens of our older people.

My family heritage has spared me from material concerns, but the legacy from my parents for which I am most grateful is the armor of Christian faith and love with which they equipped me and my brothers and sister.

My father, many years ago, set down his own personal creed, and it is one which I have striven to live by and to shape my public acts by.

"I believe," he wrote, "in the supreme worth of the individual and his right to life, liberty and the pursuit of happiness.

"I believe that every right implies a responsibility; every

opportunity, an obligation; every possession, a duty.

"I believe that the law was made for man and not man for the law; the government is the servant of the people, not their master.

"I believe in the dignity of labor, whether with head or hand; that the world owes no man a living but that it owes every man an *opportunity* to make a living.

"I believe that thrift is essential to well-ordered living and that economy is a prime requisite of a sound financial structure, whether in government, business or personal affairs.

"I believe that truth and justice are fundamental to an enduring social order.

"I believe in the sacredness of a promise, that a man's word should be as good as his bond; that character–not wealth or position–is a supreme worth.

"I believe that the rendering of useful service is the common duty of mankind and that only in the purifying fire of sacrifice is the dross of selfishness consumed and the greatness of the human soul set free.

"I believe in an all-wise and all-loving God, named by whatever name, and that the individual's highest fulfillment, greatest happiness and widest usefulness are to be found in living in harmony with his will.

"I believe that love is the greatest thing in the world; that it alone can overcome hate; that right can and will triumph over might."

What better guideposts could any public servant have? I am grateful indeed that my parents provided me with that vitally important aid, which has enabled me to find direction and meaning in life and, as it says in my favorite Bible verse, Micah 8:6, to "do justly" and to "walk humbly" with God.

Nelson A. Rockefeller served as governor of New York state for nearly fifteen years, from 1959-1973, after having been the first Governor elected to four four-year terms in the nation's history. He resigned as governor on December 18, 1973, to devote his full efforts to the chairmanship of both the Commission on Critical Choices for Americans and the National Water Quality Commission.

Mr. Rockefeller has also had long and distinguished experience on the national and international scenes, including service as Coordinator of Inter-American Affairs and Assistant Secretary of State under President Roosevelt, Chairman of the President's Commission on International Development for President Truman, and Special Assistant to the President for Foreign Affairs and Undersecretary of Health, Education and Welfare under President Eisenhower. In 1969, Governor Rockefeller carried out a Presidential Mission to Latin America for President Nixon.

Governor Rockefeller was born on July 8, 1908, at Bar Harbor, Maine, the third of six children of John D. Rockefeller, Jr., and Abby Aldrich Rockefeller. He graduated in 1926 from Lincoln School in New York City, and in 1930 from Dartmouth College, where he majored in economics and was elected to Phi Beta Kappa.

There were five children from his marriage to Mary Todhunter Clark: Rodman C.; Mrs. Lionel Coste; Steven C.; Mrs. Mary Rockefeller Strawbride; and the late Michael C. Rockefeller. On May 4, 1963, he married the former Margaretta Fitler Murphy. They have two sons, Nelson, Jr., and Mark Fitler, and make their home at Pocantico Hills, Tarrytown New York.

Margaret Chase Smith of Maine

Many nights I go home from the office or the Senate Floor tired and discouraged. There's lots of glory and prestige and limelight for a United States Senator that the public sees. But there's just as much grief and harassment and discouragement that the public doesn't see.

Of course, like everyone else I went into public service and politics with my eyes wide open. I knew that any public official is fair game for slander and smear and carping criticism. I knew that ingratitude was to be expected.

I knew that fair weather friends would turn on me when they felt I no longer served their purposes. I knew that I would be called all sorts of names, from crook on down.

I should have known that chances were good that I would even be accused of being a traitor to my country. These things I knew. But I never knew how vicious they could get and how deeply they could cut.

It is these things I think of when I'm tired and discouraged—and when I wonder if being a Senator is worth all that I put into it. These are the times when I consider quitting public life and retreating to the comforts and luxury of private life.

But these times have always been the very times when I became all the more convinced that all the sorrow, abuse,

harassment, and vilification was not too high a price or sacrifice to pay.

For it is then that I ask myself, What am I doing this for? I realize that I am doing it because I believe in certain things—things without which life wouldn't mean much to me.

This I do believe—that life has a real purpose—that God has assigned to each human being a role in life—that each of us has a purposeful task—that our individual roles are all different but that each of us has the same obligation to do the best he can.

I believe that every human being I come in contact with has a right to courtesy and consideration from me. I believe that I should not ask or expect from anyone else that which I am not willing to grant or do myself.

I believe that I should be able to take anything that I can give out. I believe that every living person has the right to criticize constructively, the right honestly to hold unpopular beliefs, the right to protest orderly, the right of independent thought.

I believe that no one has a right to own our souls except God.

I believe that freedom of speech should not be so abused by some that it is not exercised by others because of fear of smear. But I do believe that we should not permit tolerance to degenerate into indifference. I believe that people should never get so indifferent, cynical, and sophisticated that they don't get shocked into action.

I believe that we should not forget how to disagree agreeably and how to criticize constructively. I believe with all my heart that we must not become a nation of mental mutes blindly following demagogues. I believe that we should never become mental mutes with our voices silenced because of fear of criticism of what we might say.

I believe that in our constant search for security we can never gain any peace of mind until we secure our own soul. And this I do believe above all, especially in my times of greater discouragement, *that I must believe*—that I must believe in my fellowmen—that I must believe in myself—that I must believe in God—if life is to have any meaning.

Margaret Chase Smith, Showhegan, Maine, Republican, was a member of the United States House of Representatives from 1940 to 1949. She served in the United States Senate from 1949 to 1974. She is the only woman to ever have been elected to four full terms in the United States Senate. She is the first woman to have been placed in nomination for President at a national convention of a major political party.

Senator Smith made extensive trips throughout the world in 1944, 1945, 1947, 1950, 1954, 1955, 1956, 1957, and 1961. Very few people have conferred with as many leaders of nations throughout the world as has Senator Smith. She has been rated as one of America's best and most effective ambassadors of good will. For several years she has been proposed by many for the vice-presidency of the United States but has repeatedly stated that she was not interested in the vice presidency but preferred to remain in the Senate.

Senator Herman E. Talmadge of Georgia

On the fiftieth anniversary of the Declaration of Independence, Thomas Jefferson—the author of that great document—wrote to a friend and recounted the blessings of liberty.

A half century had passed since the American colonists chose to fight for freedom and founded a new nation.

Jefferson wrote to his friend that a new era had begun. All eyes, he said, are opening to the rights of man, and to the fact that man was born free—and not with a saddle on his back. At the time he wrote that letter, Jefferson's death was only a few days away.

No other American believed more in the dignity of mankind and the value of freedom. It was one of his final wishes that the Fourth of July be marked as a day of patriotic observance. Citizens would do well to read again and again the Declaration of Independence. It was the cornerstone for the American Republic.

It is also important to consider the Declaration of Independence along with the Constitution. The Declaration set forth principles to which the American people pledged their lives, fortunes, and sacred honor. The Constitution set forth the means for carrying out these principles.

Both these documents are approaching their two-hundredth year. But what they stand for is timeless. As a

nation of people, we are very often guilty of backsliding. These principles that made America great, and have kept us free, need to be reexamined and strengthened from time to time.

Thomas Jefferson no doubt would be shocked by the present state of the American Republic. He no doubt would be reminded of famous words of one of his fellow patriots, Tom Payne: "These are times that try men's souls."

The country has been torn by dissension and disorder. Principles and institutions that once were cherished by all are now scorned by many. Old-fashioned ideals of self-restraint, personal initiative—and the concepts that man works for what he gets and enjoys the fruits of his labor—have been abused. Patriotism and loyalty to God and country mean different things to different people—if they mean anything at all.

Jefferson no doubt would be greatly discouraged. But this country was not founded by men who lost heart when things were going badly. By the same token, neither our nation nor our freedom are going to be preserved today by the fainthearted.

It has often seemed to me in recent years that our nation has gone from one crisis to the next—at home and abroad. The faith of Americans in their nation and in their God is tested again and again. Yet, through it all, one characteristic of the American people has always remained firm. That is, the ability to turn adversity into advantage, and to produce a stronger nation and a more united people out of trials and tribulations.

Emerson once wrote: "When it is dark enough, men see the stars." Through crisis after crisis, domestic and foreign, the best in our people has emerged . . . *always under the sure hand of God.*

In my humble judgment, the strength of the American people can be attributed to one very important quality . . . *faith.* Faith can mean many things to many people. To some people, faith is a weapon. To others, it is a defense. To others, it is a very private, quiet, and peaceful refuge.

Regardless of its personal meaning, regardless of how each individual takes his faith and dispenses it, faith is the essence of the quality of life. Both men and nations can perhaps exist without faith . . . but not for long and never against any major challenge. A man without faith is like a ship at sea without a rudder. There is no real direction to anything he does, or anywhere he goes.

All nations and all people need faith. In my humble opinion, men need it at their side all the time. But it does seem to me that there are times when we need faith more than at other times. That is because life is so often a great test. It is a test of man's ability, intelligence, and reason, which God granted mankind alone in the creation.

But life, as much as anything else that it means, is a test of man's faith. God did not give us life only to take sustenance and to breathe for the maintenance of our bodies alone. He gave us a mind and a soul for the maintenance of faith.

Let us refresh our memory of the words of the great poet, Henry Wadsworth Longfellow in his immortal verse, "A Psalm of Life."

> Tell me not in mournful numbers,
> Life is but an empty dream!—

For the soul is dead that slumbers
And things are not what they seem.

Life is real! Life is earnest!
And the grave is not its goal;
Dust thou art, to dust returnest,
Was not spoken of the soul.

Not enjoyment, and not sorrow,
Is our destined end or way;
But to act, that each tomorrow
Find us farther than today.

Let us then be up and doing,
With a heart for any fate;
Still achieving, still pursuing,
Learn to labor and to wait.

Jesus rejected personal aggrandizement and material gain as the sole purpose of life. "Seek ye first the kingdom of God, and His righteousness," he directed in the Sermon on the Mount (Matt. 6:33).

Jesus preached also that the way would not be easy. Matthew records (10:22) these words when Jesus sent his disciples on their first missionary venture: "And ye shall be hated of all men for my name's sake: but he that endureth to the end shall be saved."

Jesus knew, and the disciples understood, that faith would lead to endurance. Faith can move mountains, open the sea, and overcome all evil. But, there must also be a measure of courage.

For my own part, I do not find the meanings of faith and courage very far apart. Aside from their accepted definitions, we can consider the two terms in this light:

One must have faith to have courage and, though this is less than desirable, it is also true that one must have courage to have faith, in this day and time.

I sometimes think, with some sadness, that a person with faith must be willing to stand alone and apart from the crowd.

The dictionary defines courage as a quality of the mind or spirit which enables a person to face difficulty, danger, or pain with firmness and without fear. In the final analysis, what is that if it is not faith?

In any event, faith and courage are characteristics that are far easier to define than to demonstrate. They are infinitely easier to picture than to possess. But nonetheless, we are each day tested for these qualities of faith and courage. It has always been, and it always will be so long as man walks this earth.

Consider the test of Abraham, whom God told to take his only son, Isaac, to Mount Moriah and offer the boy as a burnt sacrifice. This was Isaac, born to Abraham when he was one hundred years old and to his wife Sarah when she was ninety—which was in itself a blessing of God and the result of their faith. Abraham struggled. He prayed. But he obeyed—because of his faith—and made his way with his beloved son to Mount Moriah. God, of course, relented after Abraham had proved the depth of his faith.

Consider the faith of Job, a man "perfect and upright" in every way. It is impossible to measure the faith and courage of such a man. Stripped of his family, and all his worldly belongings, and plagued by disease, Job never wavered: "Naked was I born, Naked shall I die. The Lord gave, and the Lord hath taken away." Through all his suffering, Job said, "Though he slay me, yet will I trust in him."

Consider the faith and courage of Gideon, told by God to take a small force and destroy a *whole army* of Midianites. Gideon started out with 32,000, but most of them were fainthearted and fled to safer ground. He was left with just 300, but they were 300 eager to do battle for the Lord and, more importantly, they were 300 men of faith. The 300, with trumpets blaring and lamps aflame, routed the whole *Midianite* army. It was a victory won by an act of God. It was a victory of faith.

Consider also the faith of Jonathan, who put the Philistines to flight with only his armor-bearer at his side. But he had the courage of God in his heart when he told his companion it was time to go into battle. Said Jonathan: "It is time for bold action. It is time for God to work." The armor-bearer, as faithful as his leader, replied; "Do all that is in thine heart. I am with thee."

When we think on these acts and on the faith of those brave heros, perhaps we can better understand the point that the pundit was trying to make when he wrote that a religious man on his knees sees more than a philosopher on tiptoes!

In spite of whatever difficulties our nation may face today, or what may come tomorrow, let us never forget that this country was founded upon faith in God.

It was built to greatness in the adherence of our people to God's Commandments. Life was no bed of roses then. It is not now.

Paul said we are to be justified by faith and rejoice in

the hope of the glory of God. In his Epistle to the Romans, the Apostle wrote: "We glory in tribulations also; knowing that tribulation worketh patience; and patience, experience; and experience, hope" (5:3).

Each day then is a test.

In closing, recall how Henry Van Dyke suggested that each person of faith meet the new day. The poet wrote:

> Dear Lord, the newness of this day
> Calls me to an untried way:
> Let me gladly take the road,
> Give me strength to bear the load,
> Thou, my guide and helper be,
> I can travel through with Thee.

Our faith can be strengthened, it can work wonders, if we never lose sight of the sure knowledge that

> Standeth God within the shadow,
> Keeping watch upon his own.

In addition to his present service as United States senator and previously as governor of Georgia, Herman Talmadge has had a long and successful career as attorney, farmer, insurance executive, Naval officer, and businessman.

In the ninety-third Congress, Senator Talmadge has assumed new positions of increased seniority: Chairman of the Agriculture and Forestry Committee, second ranking on Finance Committee, second on Veterans Affairs Committee, second on Standards and Conduct (Ethics) Committee, Joint Committee on Internal Revenue Taxation. Talmadge served as governor of Georgia for six years, 1948-1955.

He was born August 9, 1913, near McRae, Georgia, in Telfair County. He graduated from the University of Georgia in 1936. He married Elizabeth Shingler of Ashburn, Georgia. They have two sons, Herman Talmadge, Jr., and Robert Singler Talmadge. A combat veteran of World War II, Talmadge served with the United States Navy in the South Pacific.

Senator Strom Thurmond of South Carolina

American life today is often viewed as one giant showroom. Our energies are frequently geared toward acquiring that which will make us content. Materialism in such cases becomes the object of our affections. Some use every trick in the book to get more so they can show more. Too many transfix themselves to this end.

When material comforts become our goal, we are prone to neglect the spiritual side of life. Many Americans today are finding their lives crumbling in the midst of plenty. The "something big" they have hoped and waited for often does not turn out to be what was expected.

On the surface, American life has far surpassed anything our founding fathers had in mind when they declared the inalienable right to pursue happiness.

Never has there been a time or society when so many individuals could own two or more cars; have two houses; take trips to almost any place on the globe; and send their children to the best schools money can buy. It is estimated that this year alone, Americans will spend about $115 billion for their inalienable right to pursue happiness.

While salaries and fringe benefits are going up, Americans are finding more time to indulge in their greatest fantasies. Automation has cut weekly work hours from seventy to thirty-seven in the last century. It has been estimated that by the year 2000 work weeks will be down to twenty hours. In fact, several companies across the nation have already cut back to four working days per week, creating a three-day weekend.

The result of all this is that we are witnessing an unremitting trend to allow Americans to enjoy themselves. Promises of fulfillment and contentment have become the wares of the free marketplace.

About eight million Americans will be traveling overseas this year despite the devalued dollar. Sales of radios, televisions, records, and musical instruments went up almost 190 percent between 1960 and 1971. Camping vehicles, which cost up to $30,000, have risen in number from fewer than one million eight years ago to more than four million today.

The twentieth-century frenzy to find fulfillment and satisfaction in "things" is not new. The big differnce between now and earlier times is that we possess the ability to build and produce on a massive scale. In 1800, the businessman's thirst for the so-called "good life" was tempered by the fact that he relied upon his own strengths to succeed. His hands were to him what the computer is to us. Where it took a cabinetmaker a week or longer to build a table, it takes industry just a fraction of the time.

I do not want to leave the wrong impression. I am proud of the fact that we have harnessed the human and mechanical ability to become the world's industrialized giant. The problems come when attainment of the so-called "good life" becomes an obsession to the point where God becomes secondary.

At its annual convention, the American Medical Association was told more than ten million people in this country are in dire need of treatment for acute depression.

Between 1965 and 1971, the number of young people eighteen years of age and younger undergoing psychiatric treatment rose by almost two thirds.

Suicide rates are rising and the increase is attributed in large measure to young people who cannot cope with life.

One of the most popular Broadway plays to come along in quite a while is entitled "Lemmings." It is a spoof on the last decade and grotesquely depicts the sixties as a time of mass suicide. The denouement comes with a symbolic plunge of humanity over a cliff.

Still another example of the so-called "good life" was examined in *U. S. News and World Report*. The town of Roseto, Pennsylvania, population 1,600, was once known as the "miracle town" in the early sixties. It had this distinction because no one under fifty had suffered a fatal heart attack according to records dating back to the mid-fifties. Even the older citizens averaged far fewer fatal heart attacks than the national average.

When researchers went back to this tiny town two years ago, things had changed. Two men in their early forties had died of heart attacks that year. Moreover, the rate of fatal heart attacks had been steadily increasing over the past several years.

One of the researchers was quoted in explaining this turn for the worse. "Too much has happened in ten years," he said. "People who had been living pretty much as they had for decades . . . suddenly began changing."

He said the men began commuting to better paying jobs

twenty or thirty miles away. They spent money on luxuries and sent their children away to college. He said, "The pace of living stepped up, and they had no time left to talk over their worries and satisfactions with each other."

The minister in the town pretty much summed it up when he said, "We have joined the rat race."

I am afraid that too many have joined the rat race. I sense a cold and unfeeling barrenness creeping into the American soul. I sense—to use Robinson Jeffers' words—"A gathering in the air that hates humanity."

In his quest for the so-called "good life," man often places his inherent need for God in suspended animation. When this occurs, we should expect the good life to turn sour.

One outgrowth of rampant secularism was embodied in a recently written document called "The Humanist Manifesto II." Dubbed a major social document by its subscribers, it calls for new directions of mankind, stressing a belief in mankind and his so-called "rational powers," and criticizes theistic religion as an impediment to human development.

Here is a portion of this astounding document, which, by the way, was signed by 120 philosophers, scientists, writers, religious leaders and others:

" . . . Traditional dogmatic or authoritarian religions that place revelation, God, ritual, or creed above human needs and experience do a disservice to the human species. Any account of nature should pass the test of scientific evidence; in our judgment, the dogmas and myths of traditional religions do not do so."

It goes on to say that "Promises of immortal salvation

or fear of eternal damnation are both illusory and harmful. They distract humans from present concerns, from self-actualization and from rectifying social injustices."

For many, unfortunately, this is the doctrine of the twentieth century. I would guess most people would denounce this work as hedonistic and heretical. We have not yet reached the point where a majority would put their names to such dogma.

But I wonder how many live as if religion were a myth. I wonder how many put their experiences to the scientific test; that is, if they cannot see it in black and white, they ignore it. I wonder how many live their lives with unwavering faith in God.

Man is a synthesis of the temporal and eternal, of the infinite and finite, of freedom and restraint. God has also given man the right to choose; the freedom to accomplish; and the opportunity to pursue happiness. With this, however, he has written a platform for every man to follow—the Ten Commandments.

Faith in God and faith in divine inheritance, are the keystones to a good and productive life. God has given us the tools with which to pursue the good life. At the same time, however, he expects us to temper our materialistic yearnings with the knowledge that, in the end, we will be responsible to him. It was said best in Matthew 16:26, "For what is a man profited if he shall gain the whole world, and lose his own soul."

Satisfaction and fulfillment cannot be acquired solely by money. When worldly possessions become the only ambition of man, he will fail. God expects us to have a higher purpose.

Senator Strom Thurmond was elected to the United States Senate in 1954 in a write-in campaign—the first person ever elected to a major office in the United States by this method. He is the ranking Republican on the Armed Services Committee, the senior Republican on the Veterans Affairs Committee, and a member of the Judiciary Committee. He serves on the Defense Appropriations Subcommittee and the Republican Policy Committee.

Senator Thurmond has been a farmer, lawyer, schoolteacher, athletic coach, school superintendent, state senator, judge, governor, United States Senator, and Presidential candidate.

A veteran of World War II and a Major General in the United States Army Reserve, Senator Thurmond has been awarded eighteen decorations, medals and awards, including the Legion of Merit with Oak Leaf Cluster, Bronze Star with "V," Purple Heart, Belgian Order of the Crown, and French Croix de Guerre.

Senator John Tower of Texas

I believe it of paramount importance that those of us in public life remain true to and seek guidance in the Judeo-Christian ethic. Because of the hard decisions that we face, the constant drain on our emotions, our intellect, and our energies, faith can be a rallying point and a source of strength.

In times of stress, there are two passages of Scripture that I tend to reflect on.

One is the great peroration, from Isaiah 40:31: "But they that wait upon the Lord shall renew their strength; they shall mount up with wings as eagles; they shall run, and not be weary; and they shall walk, and not faint."

The second is from Paul's Epistle to the Romans, chapter 5, verses 3-5: "And not only so, but we glory in tribulations also; knowing that tribulation worketh patience; and patience, experience; and experience hope; and hope maketh not ashamed; because the love of God is shed abroad in our hearts by the Holy Ghost which is given unto us."

John Tower was born in Houston, Texas, September 29, 1925, the son and grandson of Methodist ministers. Tower received a Bachelor's Degree in political science from South-western University in Georgetown, Texas, in 1948 and a

Master's Degree, also in political science, from Southern Methodist University in Dallas, in 1953.

Tower is a trustee of Southwestern University and of Southern Methodist University, and has honorary doctoral degrees from Southwestern University, Howard Payne College in Brownwood, Texas, and Alfred University in New York. He is a thirty-second-degree Mason and Shriner. He is past National President of Kappa Sigma Fraternity, and is a member of the American Association of University Professors, the American Legion, the Texas Historical Society, the Methodist Church, and Kiwanis.

He makes his home in Wichita Falls, with his wife, Lou and their three teenage daughters, Penny, Marian, and Jeanne.

Governor George C. Wallace of Alabama

As did many of you, I came from a family which had a close, tight-knit family unit. I suppose that the family system in our country has done more to preserve the traditions and attitudes toward prayer than any other unit—it along with the church.

My grandfather—my own immediate family spent much time with him in the summertime—was an old country doctor in the days when doctors visited patients. He lived in rural Barbour county, having moved from, you might say the urban part of the country—Clio, we call that urban. He moved to Baker Hill after his first wife passed away.

I used to visit him as a little boy, along with all the grandchildren. Each morning, as we did in our own household following his example, (but his, of course, was sometimes the longest service) we always had a prayer breakfast—every breakfast was prayer breakfast. My grandfather read from the Bible, and he gave a little lesson. Each one of us had to say a Bible verse, and we had to say a new one each day when we visited him. Sometimes I would get caught at seven and eight years old trying to hunt a new verse to memorize. Sometimes I couldn't quite memorize it in time to get to the table, and I would come up with the old faithful, "Jesus wept," which I knew and was simple.

As I grew older, I began to appreciate more and more the fact that we had grace at our table in my own home and that my mother and father both were active in the church in the little town of Clio and that my mother played the piano for the church.

Then a little later on when I came back from the Armed Services, I was involved in teaching a Sunday School class. I used to keep the pupils from jumping out the window by telling them a lot of war stories mixed along with my lesson. But we had prayer also in that class.

I do know that during War II, when I was in combat, I like all combat servicemen and others prayed. I suppose sometimes we have to reach maybe that period in our lives when we know that it's on the line, and we sometimes reach back to that reservoir of faith that was there all the time. And we used it.

I was asked to briefly say something about my recent incident that happened to me when I was literally snatched from the jaws of death.

I've never talked much publicly about it, but I do know that the reason I'm here safe and sound in mind and spirit is not only because of my own prayers but the prayers of thousands upon thousands of people in our own state and throughout the country and even throughout the world as we received so much mail from all over the world.

I was impressed at the hospital that I was in—at Holy Cross in Silver Spring, Maryland—that the doctors, every one of them, talked to me about prayer. They were devout, religious people. And so are my own doctors in Montgomery and Birmingham. I've never been as sick as I was at that time, so I had never discussed prayer with doctors, but everyone of them told me that God can help us.

Of course, God did help us through the skilled hands of surgeons and through other means. He works in various and sundry ways. But I know the value of prayer, and I know that I am alive because of my prayers and the prayers of others.

I'm not much at making testimonies publicly, but I do not believe in the new-fashioned teachings that God is dead or that when life is over here, it's all over. I think I realized that the moment I lay on the ground in Maryland. I think the first thing that went through my mind—I know it was—if it is Thy will let me live, but if not, don't let me suffer. And I looked around for my wife and she was there, because I thought that I would never see my family anymore.

I know when you get in that position, things flash before you, and you realize that when you are snatched from the jaws of death maybe if you had it all to do over again, you would be better and you would pray more. I resolved then that I would be a better man to the best of my ability if I could only live. And I am living. And I am doing my best to try to live up to that promise.

So I know that prayer is real and that we can go to our God personally. We don't have to go through anybody. Our Savior is personal. I know—I think I'm an example—that prayers are answered.

George Corley Wallace has contributed greatly to the political history of Alabama and the nation. Today he continues to serve the people in his second term as Alabama's chief executive.

Born in a small town, Clio, Alabama, August 25, 1919, his first office was president of high school senior class. His father, George Corley Wallace, Sr., was Chairman of the Barbour County Board of Revenue when he died at the age of forty. His mother, Mozell Smith Wallace, worked for the State Department of Health for twenty-two years.

After the war, Wallace was appointed assistant attorney general by Alabama Governor Chauncey Sparks. He won a seat in the legislature over two opponents in the 1946 primary when he was only twenty-seven. Wallace lost his first statewide race for the governorship in 1958. He was runner-up to Governor John Patterson, receiving over a quarter of a million votes.

National encouragement led to his entering preferential presidential primaries in Wisconsin, Indiana, and Maryland. He received as much as 43 percent of the Democratic vote in these states.

George Wallace and Lurleen Burns Wallace had four children: Bobbie Jo, Peggy Sue, George, Jr., and Janie Lee.

In January, 1971, Governor Wallace married Mrs. Cornelia Ellis Snively, a niece of former Alabama Governor James E. Folsom. She has two sons, Jim and Josh, by a previous marriage.

Governor Wallace's personal contributions to his community and state include being a Lay Leader and member of the Board of Stewards of the St. James Methodist Church. He is also a member of the American Legion, Amvets, VFW, Woodman, Moose, Elks, Civitans, Alabama PTA, Board of Directors of Alabama Pensions Institute, Inc., and Alabama Tuberculosis Association. He is a Mason and a Shriner.

Governor Jack Williams of Arizona

Someone said that religion was the opiate of the people. And someone else once said that if there were no God, man would have to invent him. These are somewhat cynical descriptions of what is more than a phenomenon and actually a fact. The religions of the world, while differing somewhat, have always been realistically necessary for the survival of mankind.

Government is seldom as successful as a religion, although the shepherd king is said to have been the source of both ruler and religious leader.

It seems to me that so-called conventional religion has a tendency to water itself down to a point where it becomes so weak it cannot survive. I am speaking of contemporary religion as demonstrated by our Christian or Judeo-Christian sects.

I was amazed in Israel to see the strict Jews and the nonsectarian Jews living side by side. But the Jews who followed the ancient biblical tenets represent survival over centuries of persecution.

The new nonsectarian and almost nonreligious young Jew in the Holy Land, is a new phenomenon, who may be only a tiny mark in the pages of history. I do not know. I only know that continual compromise whittles away strength, and without strength and purpose and desire, a

religion, a sect, and even a people face annihilation.

Today, the phenomenon of our age in this country is the development and growth of the fundamentalist churches—the strict ones. Many of the large denominations that are not fundamentalist, or Bible-oriented, are losing membership and support. They are identifiable by the position of their clergy who take a permissive position on what the Bible churches call sin.

It is possible that people prefer to know when they are sinning. In fact, I once observed that the worst sin of all is to sin and not know it. If this be worth consideration, then a church or denomination that makes it easy to sin is a tool of the devil, to use one of the phrases of the more fundamentalist sects.

(May I hastily add for the purposes of this visit, I am not taking sides in this matter.)

I made a vow many years ago that when at all possible I would attend a church on Sunday. My youngsters went unprotestingly to church on Sunday, because their father took them, and it was just assumed that one went to church on Sunday morning. I'm sure that I did shake them up a bit one year when, after going to our own church, we paid visits to a great variety of other churches. Our church had a 9:30 service, and then we took in the 11:00 service of other denominations. I found it educational and interesting, but I'm afraid at a tender age, the youngsters were not so impressed.

Of late, I go to many different churches. The other Sunday I attended a small one, without a pastor and without a choir.

Sitting in front of me, three youngsters, with their parents, let the service wash over them. Three blonde kids, ages four, five, and seven. Two girls and a boy. Tow-heads, all; two with brown eyes and one with blue eyes. Hair cuts, a homemade job, all the same style, but cut! Tennis shoes and short socks. Homemade frocks for the girls, Levis for the little boy. The dresses were simple sacks, with different borders at the bottom, hanging straight and shapeless from the shoulders.

I admire the mother and father who brought them to church. And I wanted to praise the interim lay pastor, who took his message from the Sermon on the Mount.

Perhaps the youngsters weren't listening, but as the years go on they will have some faint memory of those words of the most-repeated sermon ever preached.

Governor Williams was born October 29, 1909, in Los Angeles, California. He was married to the former Vera May in 1942. They have three children: Richard, Hermosa Beach, California; Michael, LaJolla, California; and Mrs. Ron Newcome, Kirtland, Washington.

He was employed by Radio KOY in 1929 and became an announcer and newscaster. He was advanced to program director in the 20's and became part owner of the station in 1948. His executive positions included that of president until he sold the station shortly before becoming governor.

Jack Williams entered public life as a member of the Board of Trustees of Phoenix Elementary School District No. 1. He used his vote to end segregation in the schools of that district. He was elected mayor of Phoenix in 1956. Jack Williams was first elected governor in 1966. He is now in his third term.

Epilogue

Religion and politics inevitably mix in the life of a Christian. Genuine commitment to the lordship of Christ pervades every sector of life—politics as well as prayer, patriotism as well as piety, and citizenship in the government as well as membership in the church. The dynamics of the Christian faith nurture a life-style which embraces responsible participation in the political process.

True religion, according to the Bible, consists of an unconditional love for God which finds expression in caring service to others. For the contemporary Christian, faithful adherence to the scriptural admonitions related to helping the helpless, feeding the hungry, caring for the ill, eradicating discrimination, and rehabilitating the criminal will surely require some long-term interworking with various structures of government. The larger goals of such political participation include influencing the development of a society characterized by equitable laws, a passion for peace, guarantees of freedom, and justice for all.

Politics is the art of government. The methods by which governmental revenues are collected and allocated, foreign and domestic policies formulated, and legislative proposals enacted are unmistakably political. The morality or immorality of the process is dependent upon the persons involved in it.

When the religion is Christianity, politics and religion can only be separated to the detriment of both. Politics provides the Christian a means of social involvement with tremendous potential for affecting significant change, attacking evil, and establishing justice. Religion provides politics the kind of motivation, goals, methods, and conscience which can make the system moral as well as effective. The Christian mixes politics and religion for the good of humanity and the glory of God.

C. WELTON GADDY
Director of Christian Citizenship Development
Christian Life Commission of the
Southern Baptist Convention